THE MAKING OF WALES

JOHN DAVIES

CADW: WELSH HISTORIC MONUMENTS

SUTTON PUBLISHING LIMITED

For Anna

First Published in the United Kingdom in 1996 by
Alan Sutton Publishing Limited, an imprint of Sutton Publishing Limited
Phoenix Mill, Thrupp, Stroud, Gloucestershire
in association with
Cadw: Welsh Historic Monuments
Crown Building, Cathays Park, Cardiff CF1 3NQ

Paperback edition first published in 1999

British Library Cataloguing-in-Publication Data

A catalogue record for this book is available from the British Library
ISBN 0-7509-2176-5

ALAN SUTTON™ and SUTTON™ are the
trade marks of Sutton Publishing Limited

Production Editing: David M. Robinson and Diane Williams
Design: Joanna Griffiths
Principal Photography: Paul Highnam, Jonathan Pimlott, Harry Williams
Maps and Plans: Cartographic Services, Welsh Office

Colour Separation by Yeo Valley Graphics
Printed in Great Britain by Butler & Tanner, Frome, Somerset

CONTENTS

PREFACE AND ACKNOWLEDGEMENTS

The invitation to write this book was for me the cause of both trepidation and delight. The trepidation arose from the realization that the history of the landscape is the history of everything, and thus the task before me was hugely daunting. The delight arose from the realization that the commission meant that I was obliged systematically to visit sites and look at buildings, a pleasure I had pursued in a disorganized way ever since, as a six-year old, my father took me to see the Maendy hillfort above Treorci.

'Everything', wrote W. G. Hoskins in his celebrated volume of 1955, 'is older than we think'. He was directing his argument specifically against the notion — then widely held — that the countryside looks the way it does chiefly as a result of the parliamentary enclosures of the late eighteenth and early nineteenth centuries. Hoskins pushed back the date of major landscape-making by over six hundred years and emphasized in particular the role of the assarters — the tree clearers — of the twelfth and thirteenth centuries. The tendency now is to push everything much further back. Oliver Rackham has demonstrated that the landscape of the Lizard Peninsula in Cornwall 'has altered little in a thousand years'. 'To convert millions of acres of wildwood into farmland', he asserts, 'is unquestionably the greatest achievement of our ancestors'. The clearing began in the Mesolithic era and accelerated hugely in the Neolithic, Bronze and Iron Ages. Thus, huge strides in the making of the landscape had been taken long before Wales tiptoed into the historical record in the first century A.D. To a great extent, therefore, the making of Wales is a prehistoric phenomenon and thus the names of its early makers are wholly unknown to us.

Even with the dawn of history, the paucity of written records means that the makers of Wales remain anonymous. We can surmise that the Roman frontier in Wales was planned by Julius Frontinus, the governor of the province of Britannia from A.D. 74 to 78, but we do not know the names of those who dug initial ramparts and ditches at Gelligaer, built walls at Caerleon and paved the hundreds of miles of Roman roads. Even when documentation becomes more plentiful, the actual makers continue to elude us. We know that Master James of St George designed Edward I's great castles, that Telford and Jessop designed Pont Cysyllte, and that Rickards designed Cardiff's City Hall, but who dug the foundations and who applied the mortar? To write of the makers of Wales is to pay tribute to a vastly long succession of users of axes, spades and trowels, to shapers of timber, to quarriers of stone and slate, and, in more recent times, to drivers of bulldozers and mechanical diggers. We can name hardly any of them. Yet they are commemorated, for the landscape itself is their memorial.

In writing the book, I have gathered many obligations. My first debt is to John Carr and to Glanmor Williams, who suggested that I should write it. The officers of Cadw, in particular David Robinson and Diane Williams, have shown remarkable kindness and patience. The text was read in whole or in part by Rees Davies, John Hilling, Jeremy Knight, Frances Lynch Llewelyn, William Manning and Peter Wakelin, and I am grateful for their constructive suggestions. Many museums, agencies and individuals have helped with illustrations, but in this respect I should particularly like to thank Jeremy Lowe, Chris Musson of the Royal Commission on the Ancient and Historical Monuments of Wales, and the Wales Tourist Board photographic libary. The layout was prepared by Joanna Griffiths, the maps and plans by Peter Lawrence, and the book has benefited from their talents. At Alan Sutton, Roger Thorp and Jane Singleton have been supportive throughout. Above all, as always, my greatest debt is to my wife, Janet Mackenzie Davies, and to my children. To dedicate the book to the eldest of them is the greatest delight of all.

Opposite: *The 'Roman Steps' near Harlech in Gwynedd mark a mountain pass of considerable antiquity (Harry Williams Photographic Library).*

PROLOGUE

The Blorenge near Abergavenny is the place to start. This mass of heather, bracken and whinberries thrusts out above the Usk valley; it marks the north-eastern corner of the south Wales coalfield and dominates the only area where the coal valleys are in close — if uneasy — contact with rich agricultural land.

The twentieth century is very visible here. Looking to the east from the Blorenge, the eye is drawn to the modern roadway, the A40, now a semi-motorway, which gashes its route across the green lushness of central Monmouthshire. To the west, the Anacomp building rears up above Brynmawr, its angular bulk housing one of the world's most modern computer software factories. The second half of the nineteenth century is here too: the Newport to Hereford railway (1854), the Big Pit on the upper reaches of the river Llwyd (1860), and Forgeside, Blaenavon, where Gilchrist and Thomas pioneered the smelting of phosphoric ores (1877). So is the first part of that century: the Blorenge overlooks the great cirque of Llanwenarth, where evidence of the vanished community celebrated by Alexander Cordell is immediately apparent. Equally apparent is the location of the tramroad which slid down the mountain to the canal below; the canal is still there and I can see holiday-makers clambering over the decks of the barges moored at the Govilon quay. And a very different early nineteenth century is represented beyond Abergavenny where Clytha House, Wales's finest Greek revival building, edges into view.

The eighteenth century has left memorable imprints, including the landscaped park at Coldbrook and those of the side streets of Abergavenny which 1960s planners fortunately neglected to demolish. The seventeenth century had its demolishers too; far away to the east lie the ruins of the great Yellow Tower of Gwent, partially undermined following the Civil War. The demolition marked the final demise of an old world, and the arrival of a new world is represented by the erection in the 1690s of chapels at Llanwenarth and Abergavenny, harbingers of a great building crusade. Evidence of the sixteenth century is less immediately obvious; but it is there, for many of the substantial farmhouses which dot the landscape of eastern Monmouthshire stand on sixteenth-century foundations.

Despite the partial ruination of the great fifteenth-century Yellow Tower, the fortified palace of the Herberts at Raglan, it remains a dramatic symbol of the wealth and power of the lords of the March. A more appealing reminder of fifteenth-century Wales lies in the hills to the north. The Grwyne joins the Usk below the mistletoe-encrusted trees of Cwrt-y-gollen and the line of the Grwyne valley can be followed until it melts into the blue haze of the Black Mountains. Just below the haze lies Patrisio church, with its splendid rood screen; the church is not visible from the Blorenge, but to know that Patrisio is there and to imagine it brings a rich contentment. The Blorenge offers a fine view of Abergavenny Priory, the necropolis of some of the leading lords of the south-eastern March. Now bereft of its conventual buildings, its fourteenth-century tower stands serenely in a whirl of traffic. The earlier medieval centuries are represented too, with masonry castles at Abergavenny, Crickhowell and Tretower, and a rash of mottes and ringworks, among them Bryngwyn, Penrhos, Newcastle, Betws Newydd and Dingestow.

Over thirty parishes are visible from the Blorenge, and more than twenty of them bear *llan* names. Some commemorate the great saints of Christendom — Mary, Peter and Michael among them — but the majority honour saints of the Celtic Church, with Cadog, Teilo and Dewi in the lead. These *llannau* indicate the desire, from the fifth century onwards, to imprint the landscape with the names of the founders of Christianity in Wales. That Christianity emerged from the Roman occupation, and there, on the banks of the Usk, at the foot of the Blorenge, lies *Gobannium*, the Roman fort controlling the point where the Usk emerges from its narrow valley into the plain.

To the north-west, there is another fortification — Crug Hywel on Table Mountain — an Iron Age hillfort overlooking the confluence of the Grwyne Fawr and the Grwyne Fechan. And beyond, in serried ranks up to the summit of Pen Allt-mawr, are cairns, the burial places of the Bronze Age people who settled in these noble uplands. But the features which dominate the view from the Blorenge are fields — thousands of them — and hedgerows — hundreds of miles of them. The turning of the forests of the Usk valley and its flanking hills into fields was a long, long process. It began 6,000 and more years ago and

The Iron Age hillfort of Crug Hywel, situated atop Table Mountain (Crown Copyright: The Royal Commission on the Ancient and Historical Monuments of Wales).

Right: *The Blorenge and its surrounding landscape: a map illustrating places mentioned in the text (Cartographic Services, Welsh Office, from a base by Lovell Johns).*

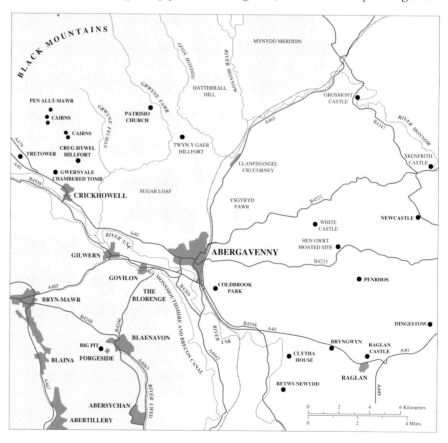

there, beyond Crickhowell, I can see the grave of some of the pioneer field-creators. This is the Gwernvale chambered tomb, erected by Neolithic people, and last used as a burial site about 3500 B.C.

Thus the view from the Blorenge offers a panorama of a palimpsest — a landscape upon which at least two hundred generations of human beings have left layer upon layer of impressions. The countryside has traditionally been considered wholly natural, in contrast with the artificiality of the town. Yet there is nowhere in twentieth-century Wales which is in any sense primeval. Everywhere the results of the labours of human beings are evident. In consequence, the notion of the naturalness of the countryside has been replaced by an insistence that, by the twentieth century — and indeed, long before the twentieth century — the countryside had become as artificial as the town. Rural Wales, like urban and industrial Wales, it is argued, is the product of the human makers of Wales. This argument can give rise to the belief that, as the landscape is man-made, there is no limit to what man can do with it, for to modify the landscape is merely to continue a long and hallowed tradition. Yet the panorama from the Blorenge is not solely the result of human ambition and design. It has come into existence through the interaction between the natural world and human activity. Furthermore, its major features are vastly older than any human activity, for this landscape was in the making long before — millions of years before — the first human set foot upon it. The Old Red Sandstone which underlies the soil in the borderlands of Monmouthshire and Powys was laid down between 370 and 415 million years ago. Thus, while the argument that the countryside is a human artefact is an important antidote to the anti-urban bias implicit in many landscape studies, it is an argument which should be tempered with humility. Human beings are the co-makers of the landscape; in addition, they are its custodians — custodians not only of its beauty but also of its meaning.

I walk down from the Blorenge to the upper reaches of the Clydach Gorge, a place resonant with meaning. On the way, I suck the juice of the mountain's fat whinberries and nibble the grain of the wayside wild oats. At the top of the gorge, reddish water rich in iron drips from the rock and a narrow vein of coal emerges on the cliff side. I drink the iron water and chew a little of the coal. I am in communion with the land.

A Norman castle motte was raised at Tretower in the last years of the eleventh century — so began the transformation of economic life, with the most profitable lands absorbed into the Anglo-Norman manorial structure. In the fifteenth century, a well-appointed courtyard house was built by Sir Roger Vaughan (d. 1471). Tretower Court was to serve more than ten generations of the Vaughan family through to the early eighteenth century.

A Palaeolithic 'handaxe' of about 125,000 B.C. found at Rhossili on the Gower peninsula. The object was a chance find, but it provides some evidence for the very earliest presence of man in the Welsh landscape (National Museum & Gallery Cardiff).

THE EARLIEST MAKERS

PALAEOLITHIC AND MESOLITHIC WALES

APPROXIMATE DATES

Lower Palaeolithic:	Earliest Man – 120,000 B.C.
Middle Palaeolithic:	120,000 – 60,000 B.C.
Upper Palaeolithic:	60,000 – 8000 B.C.
Mesolithic:	8000 – 4500 B.C.

A human tooth, dating to around 250,000 B.C., discovered at Pontnewydd Cave near St Asaph in north-east Wales: its owner has been hailed as 'the first Welshman' (National Museum & Gallery Cardiff).

The landscape upon which the original makers of Wales made their mark was that which emerged following the retreat of the glaciers, over 12,000 years ago. There had been human beings in Wales long before the last of the Ice Ages, known as the Devensian (120,000 to 12,000 B.C.), for a human tooth discovered at the Pontnewydd Cave near St Asaph has been dated to around 250,000 B.C. The cave is the only site of the Lower Palaeolithic yet discovered in Wales and is the most north-westerly of its period in Europe. The Devensian Ice Age was punctuated by several warmer periods such as that around 60,000 B.C., the probable date of the stone axes discovered at Coygan cave near Laugharne, Wales's only indubitable site of the Middle Palaeolithic period. The most remarkable site of the Upper Palaeolithic period is Goat's Hole Cave in Gower, the burial place of the 'Red Lady of Paviland'. The 'Red Lady' is in fact the skeleton of a young man, who lived around 25,000 B.C. He was buried with a number of ivory ornaments in earth strongly impregnated with iron oxide, the first example in Wales of ritual burial which eventually looms so large in the archaeological record. From broadly the same era, there is evidence of human activity at Ffynnon Beuno and Cae Gwyn, caves near Tremeirchion in Flintshire. It consists of flint implements — scrapers, blades and chisels — more delicate and specialized than those used by earlier peoples.

About a thousand years after the death of the 'Red Lady', the Devensian Ice Age entered its most severe phase, and for the following 10,000 years the whole of Wales, apart from the southernmost fringes, was covered with ice. The fringes may have had human inhabitants, but the current view is that there was a hiatus in human settlement until the Late Glacial period (12,000 to 8000 B.C.), when the ice was relaxing its grip. It was then that continuous human settlement began in Wales with the inward movement of people of the

Goat's Hole Cave on the south Gower coast, the burial place of the 'Red Lady of Paviland'. The lady was in fact a man aged about 25 who was ceremonially buried in this cave around 25,000 B.C.

Two of the flint tools recovered from Goat's Hole Cave (National Museum & Gallery Cardiff).

later Upper Palaeolithic era. Settlement is believed to have been the result of movement across the land bridge which until about 8000 B.C. linked Britain with mainland Europe. Stone tools of the period have been discovered, for example, at Hoyle's Mouth Cave near Tenby. With the climate still very cold, their makers would have lived in a tundra-like landscape. Their fellow mammals included reindeer and bison, animals whose gregariousness would have supplied hunters with a ready source of food.

The climate improved rapidly following the final retreat of the ice. From about 7000 to 2500 B.C., temperatures were between 3 and 5 degrees Fahrenheit higher than today. These were the Boreal and Atlantic periods and were characterized by the growth of trees. Pollen analysis allows the chronology and geography of tree growth to be worked out in remarkable detail. Juniper established itself first, followed by birch, pine, hazel, elm, oak, alder, lime and ash. Cors Caron on the Teifi was the first site in Wales to be examined for pollen and is a key site in the history of pollen studies. Radio-carbon dating enables archaeologists to assert that hazel trees first grew at Tregaron in about 7800 B.C. The whole of Wales below 2,000 feet (610m) came to be covered by a thick canopy of trees. Open grassland was restricted to the very highest land, thus robbing the reindeer and the bison of their feeding grounds. Their place was taken by a far less gregarious woodland fauna — red deer, swine, hare and wild oxen.

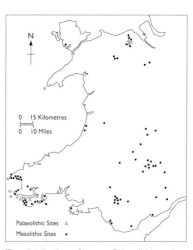

The distribution of known Palaeolithic and Mesolithic sites in Wales.

An outline chronology of landscape development in Wales (After Caseldine 1990, and Linnard in Owen 1989).

Calendar Years	Pollen Zone	Climatic Period	Archaeological Period	Climate	Vegetation	Trees Percent
1000 — AD/BC	VIII	Sub-Atlantic	Modern / Medieval / Early Christian / Romano-British / Iron Age	Deterioration	Reforestation / Forest shrinkage / Oak-birch-beech-alder	
1000 / 2000	VIIb	Sub-Boreal	Bronze Age	Stable	Mixed oak forest and alder woods	
3000			Neolithic			
4000	VIIa	Atlantic		Climatic Optimum		
5000			Mesolithic			
6000	VI	Boreal		Rapid Amelioration	Oak-alder / Pine-hazel	
7000	V				Pine-hazel-birch	
8000	IV	Pre-Boreal			Birch-pine	
	III			Cold	'Park-tundra'	
9000	II	Late Glacial	Upper Palaeolithic	Cool	Tundra	
	I					

Footprints representing at least three people who walked across the mud of the Usk estuary over 6,500 years ago. These people probably belonged to one of the bands of Mesolithic hunter-gatherers who had begun to take advantage of the rich natural resources available around the shores of Wales at this time (National Museum & Gallery Cardiff).

This was the setting for the Mesolithic people of about 8000 to 4500 B.C. Mesolithic sites far outnumber those of the Palaeolithic period, indicating not only the destruction of the latter by ice sheets, but also suggesting that the more favourable climate of early post-glacial times permitted a greater density of population. Most of the Mesolithic sites discovered in Wales are near the present coastline, but as many low-lying areas were drowned following the retreat of the ice, it is likely that numerous sites, particularly of the early part of the period, now lie beneath the sea. The most celebrated Mesolithic site is that at Nab Head near Marloes in Pembrokeshire, which has yielded masses of stone implements, including scoops for scraping the flesh of shellfish from their shells. The most interesting discovery is the 'Nab Head Venus'; a carved piece of shale some 4 inches (10.2cm) long, it has been interpreted as either a phallus or a female figure.

The pollen record suggests that tree clearance occurred in parts of Wales during the Mesolithic period, presumably the result of the deliberate use of fire to create forest glades and then to modify the landscape. Later during that era, when the Welsh uplands experienced increasingly heavy rainfall, the combination of treelessness and waterlogging led to a rampant growth of peat which, even without further human intervention, would have inhibited the growth of trees. The Mesolithic burnings were therefore the first major example of the impact of the human makers of Wales. The Blorenge, which is about 1,800 feet (550m) above sea level, was almost certainly forested in the mid Mesolithic age. It is now moorland, as are great tracts of Wales. The moorlands are generally considered to be a wholly natural landscape, but they are essentially man-made, although the process of making them extended well beyond the Mesolithic period.

While climatic change in Britain — and in Europe generally — led to the forest cultures of the Mesolithic people, the reaction elsewhere was different.

In the Near East, where higher temperatures led to the spread of deserts, the reaction was to invent agriculture. The early farmers of the Near East practised slash-and-burn tactics, which rapidly exhaust the fertility of the soil. They were therefore obliged to move, and archaeologists posit a gradual movement of farmers from Anatolia to Greece and the Danube valley and eventually across Europe, reaching Britain by about 4500 B.C. By growing crops and tending animals, human beings can sustain themselves in far greater numbers than could the hunter-gatherers of the Mesolithic period. In a few generations, the incoming farmers could have had descendants numerous enough to overwhelm the sparse Mesolithic inhabitants. The westward-moving farmers may well have been speakers of Indo-European languages, and it is conceivable that the ancestor of Brittonic (the language spoken in southern Britain at the time of the Roman invasion, itself the ancestor of the Welsh language) was spoken in this island over 6,000 years ago.

The promontory at Nab Head near Marloes in Pembrokeshire — the most celebrated Mesolithic site yet discovered in Wales. Excavations here have yielded masses of stone implements used by the fishing and hunting community which used this site as a base for exploitation of the coastal landscape. An Iron Age promontory fort can be seen on the right of the headland in this view (Crown Copyright: The Royal Commission on the Ancient and Historical Monuments of Wales, 905545-18).

The Neolithic makers of Wales, as both pastoralists and agrarianists, needed open spaces on a far greater scale than those required by their hunter-gatherer predecessors. The main tools for clearing woodland were smoothly polished stone axes. On softwoods, such axes can be as effective as steel. This example, from Aberavon in south Wales, was found with part of its birch-wood handle still intact (National Museum & Gallery Cardiff).

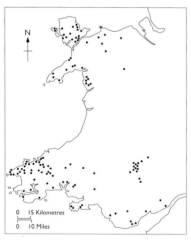

The distribution of Neolithic chambered tombs in Wales. The variety in their form of construction suggests there were eventually a number of regional Neolithic cultures across the Welsh landscape.

Opposite: *The megalithic chambered tomb of Pentre Ifan, set on the edge of the Preseli Mountains in south-west Wales. It is one of more than a hundred and fifty such tombs raised by the Neolithic people of Wales.*

THE MAKERS BECOME FARMERS

NEOLITHIC WALES

Until the late 1950s, the Neolithic period — the age of farmers lacking metal — was considered to have lasted for about 400 years (about 2300 to 1900 B.C.). The radio-carbon dating revolution has resulted in its sixfold expansion, from about 4500 to 1900 B.C. The Neolithic makers of Wales can thus be seen to have operated over a far greater timespan than was once thought, and their impact should be visualized as a series of slow but cumulative changes. As both pastoralists and agrarianists, the Neolithic farmers would have needed open spaces on a far greater scale than had their hunter-gatherer predecessors. Thus the attack upon the wildwood gathered pace. The early farmers would have begun with occasional clearings, but by about 3000 B.C. exploitation became more intense as the population increased and as grazing by animals inhibited tree regeneration. Hence clearings evolved into extensive open spaces.

Unlike their predecessors in the Palaeolithic and Mesolithic periods, the Neolithic people had implements of polished stone. On softwoods, a polished stone axe can be as effective as steel. In an experiment in Denmark, three men using stone axes cleared 600 square yards (500sq m) of birch wood in four hours. The volcanic rocks of Wales were a useful source of raw material for the making of axes. There was quarrying in the Preseli Mountains, but the most significant site is that of Y Graig Lwyd on Mynydd Penmaenmawr, east of Bangor. There was much activity there in the centuries after 3000 B.C., when the earliest quarrymen of Gwynedd were shaping the hard stone into rough-outs. Axes of Penmaenmawr stone have been found in many parts of Britain and their distribution suggests the ability of the people of the Neolithic period to organize trade on an extensive scale.

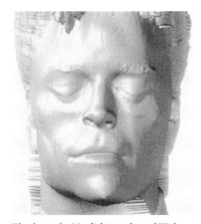

The face of a Neolithic maker of Wales: this computer image was derived from the skull of a man, dating to about 3500 B.C., excavated at Penywyrlod chambered tomb near Talgarth.

Further proof of the wide-ranging contacts of the Neolithic communities is provided by their most celebrated activity — the building of megalithic tombs. Wales has over a hundred and fifty such tombs. The variety in their construction suggests that by the middle of the Neolithic period there were in Wales a number of regional cultures. In the south-east, tombs such as those at Tinkinswood and St Lythans in the Vale of Glamorgan have affinities with those in neighbouring English counties and belong to the so-called Cotswold-Severn group. Those of the western coastlands are more various, but the most assured are the 'portal dolmens' with high stone doorways and huge capstones like those at Tan y Muriau on Llŷn and Dyffryn Ardudwy just south of Harlech. Such tombs are related to those in south-east Ireland. At a later date, the magnificent passage grave at Barclodiad y Gawres (the giantess's apron) on the island of Anglesey shows similar links to the great tombs of the Boyne valley. The general distribution of these tombs indicates that their builders were accustomed to sailing the western sea routes.

The tombs were used for communal burial, often over many generations; Tinkinswood, for example, contained parts of at least fifty individuals. The face of one of those buried at Penywyrlod near Talgarth has been reconstructed; if alive today, his handsome features would make him very welcome as a son-in-law. Yet to call the structures tombs may be to overstress their funereal role. Bodies were certainly placed in them, but as they were the centres of communal ritual, they had wider functions. It is believed that they were the work of fairly egalitarian clans and that the tomb — or the cromlech,

The megalithic tomb at Parc le Breos, Gower, belongs to the Cotswold-Severn tradition of such monuments. Off the narrow passage leading into the front of the tomb, there are two transeptal chambers to each side. A muddled and disarticulated collection of bones, representing up to twenty-four individuals, was recovered from the tomb.

to use a more traditional term — was the focus of the life of a community of a few dozen families, although it would have been built through the joint efforts of several such communities. It is estimated that at least two hundred men would have been needed to crown the Tinkinswood cromlech with its capstone — the largest in Britain. Evidence of the dwellings of the cromlech builders is far less plentiful. At Clegyr Boia near St Davids, two huts of timber and daub with wall footings of stone have been discovered; the site also contained pottery with Irish affinities. And at Llandegai near Bangor evidence for a great three-roomed wooden house has been found. The scarcity of known Neolithic settlements does not in itself mean that our knowledge of them will always be slight, for hardly one in a hundred of the potential sites has as yet been excavated.

Barclodiad y Gawres — the giantess's apron — is a magnificent passage grave which was related to similar structures in south-east Ireland. The restored mound of the tomb is situated in a spectacular coastal location overlooking Trecastell Bay on the island of Anglesey.

From about 2500 B.C., burial traditions changed from communal to individual graves. The body was often accompanied by elaborate grave goods, including a distinctive form of pottery vessel known as a 'beaker'. Such 'beakers' could be elaborately decorated, like this example from Llanharry in Glamorgan, and were perhaps prized items of status (National Museum & Gallery Cardiff).

THE MAKERS DISCOVER METALS

EARLY AND MIDDLE BRONZE AGE WALES

If the Neolithic period is defined as the era of communities of farmers using stone tools, then it did not come to an end in Wales until well after 2000 B.C., when some metal tools probably came within reach of the entire population. But there were metal objects in Wales from about 2500 B.C. onwards — objects made of copper initially, and later, as it was realized that copper is hardened by the addition of tin, objects made of bronze.

The coming of bronze was traditionally believed to mark the settlement of Britain by a new people, the 'Beaker Folk', so called because of the highly distinctive type of pot in use among them. By the later twentieth century, however, views had changed. While archaeologists agree that a new racial type — robust and broad-skulled — may be found in many of the burial sites containing beakers, it is now believed that there were no mass invasions; rather were there inward movements of small groups of people which were not sufficiently numerous to threaten the existence of locally established communities. Until fairly recently, the dominant feature of the prehistory of Britain was believed to be a sequence of invasions, for changes in material culture were seen as the result of a succession of migrations. The current tendency is to deprecate the notion of abrupt change and to emphasize the continuance and development of existing society. The increasing number of individual rather than communal burials, however, suggests that by about 2000 B.C. society was becoming dominated by an aristocratic, perhaps priestly, caste. There is some evidence that communities were more volatile and nomadic than they had been before, and a growing distinction between ceremonial and burial sites may be discerned. Yet communal burial was already in decline in the late Neolithic period, and the existence of henges, especially the early example at Llandegai near Bangor, indicates that the

In this reconstruction of a cist burial from Brymbo in north-east Wales, the skeleton of an Early Bronze Age maker of Wales is seen accompanied by a 'beaker' and a flint flake knife — doubtless symbols of his rank and status in life (National Museum & Gallery Cardiff).

extensive ritual sites of the Bronze Age had precedents over a thousand years earlier.

In terms of the making of Wales, the main significance of the Bronze Age is that the transformation of the landscape was being continued and intensified. Landscape transformation was assisted by the development of the plough, the discovery of the wheel and, possibly, by the adoption of manuring practices. The growing importance of metal tools would have enhanced the domination of man over the landscape, and in Wales evidence for the exploitation of natural mineral resources is increasing with the recognition that copper mining on the Great Orme, in Anglesey, and also in Cardiganshire, was beginning shortly after 2000 B.C. Every new piece of evidence strengthens the belief that the landscape was more highly developed and that society was more structured than was previously believed. Above all, population densities were much greater; indeed they may well have been a hundred times higher than the levels suggested a generation ago.

Population growth puts pressure on land. In the favourable climate of the Early and Middle Bronze Age, new settlements could be created by pushing cultivation up to ever higher altitudes. Today, it seems incredible that cereals were ever grown near the source of the Brenig river in the Hiraethog Mountains over 1,650 feet (500m) above sea level; yet pollen analysis shows that wheat and barley were grown there in the Middle Bronze Age. The upland settlements where they were grown were abandoned as a result of the deteriorating climate of the Late Bronze and early Iron Ages, and the monuments their inhabitants created have therefore survived relatively unscathed. This is especially true of the high ground above the coastal fringe

The landscape of the upper Brenig valley contains a wide range of Bronze Age cairns, barrows and ritual monuments, forming a cemetery which appears to have been of great significance from about 2000 to 1500 B.C. This ring cairn on the edge of the Brenig reservoir was reconstructed after excavation. It remained in use throughout the life of the cemetery (Mick Sharp Photographic Library).

Bronze Age cairns were frequently sited in prominent locations, like these three large examples at the summit of Foel Trigarn in the Preseli Mountains. In the Iron Age, the cairns were surrounded by the ramparts and ditches of a hillfort (Crown Copyright: The Royal Commission on the Ancient and Historical Monuments of Wales).

These prominent standing stones at Penrhos Feilw on Holyhead Island, Anglesey, were doubtless of ritual or memorial significance in the Bronze Age landscape.

of Merioneth (in Ardudwy and on the slopes of Cadair Idris), and in the uplands of Breconshire and on the Glamorgan ridges. Thus an appreciation of the work of the Bronze Age makers of Wales means visiting sites on the high moorland. Dartmoor has been described as a complete Bronze Age landscape. The same could be said of many areas of upland Wales.

The upper Brenig valley offers the finest display, partly because detailed work in the mid 1970s, prior to the creation of the Brenig reservoir, uncovered almost the totality of the monuments. Indeed, this underlines a fundamental fact about archaeology: what we know depends not upon what there is, but upon where we have looked. Other areas where cairns stand out against the sky include the Kerry hills, the moors above the Elan valley and the Preseli Mountains, in particular the three large cairns on Foel Trigarn. Even more impressive is Y Gop south of Prestatyn; 40 feet (12.2m) high and 330 feet (100m) wide, it is the largest Bronze Age cairn in Wales.

Some Bronze Age memorials are marked by tall, isolated monoliths up to 13 feet (4m) high — at Cefn Graeanog near Llanllyfni, for example, or at Battle near Brecon. Concentrations of such standing stones — sometimes, but not always, in conjunction with burials — have a distribution pattern which provides further evidence of Bronze Age upland settlement. Among the most intriguing of Wales's stone circles is that at Ysbyty Cynfyn in the upper Rheidol valley. Millennia after its construction, it came to contain a church and churchyard, one of the many examples of the reuse of the monuments of one age by another. In terms of stone circles, Wales has nothing to offer comparable with the astonishing remains at Carnac in Brittany where there are almost 3,000 menhirs. Nevertheless, the twenty stones at Cerrig Duon near the source of the Tawe or the sixteen stones at Gors Fach in the Preseli Mountains offer an evocative experience to the seekers of the Bronze Age makers of Wales.

Recent interpreters of Bronze Age communities argue that, by about 2000 B.C., much of southern Britain consisted of a series of quasi-states with clearly defined borders. Great monuments such as Silbury Hill and Stonehenge suggest that the most powerful of such states were located on the Downs of Wessex. The eighty blue stones at Stonehenge were conveyed there from the Preseli Mountains, suggesting perhaps that the mountains had mystical significance. Wales offers virtually no evidence of human settlements of the Early and Middle Bronze Ages, although it is possible that burial cairns were constructed over what had previously been habitations. The closest we can get to the domestic life of Wales's Bronze Age people is their burnt mounds — stones used to heat pools in which meat was probably cooked, although the pools may have been the Bronze Age equivalent of a sauna. Among the best examples are those at Cefn Tryfar, east of Clynnog Fawr, and others almost certainly remain to be discovered.

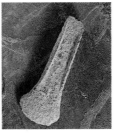

Tools and weapons made of bronze became increasingly common in Wales from about 2000 B.C. This example of an Early Bronze Age 'flanged' axe comes from Neath (National Museum & Gallery Cardiff).

The Early Bronze Age 'kerb circle' at Moel Tŷ Uchaf near Corwen occupies a commanding hilltop position with outstanding views across the landscape in all directions. 'Kerb circles' are just one of the many variants of the ritual and funerary monuments to be found in the relic features of the Bronze Age landscape in Wales (Mick Sharp Photographic Library).

THE MAKERS CREATE FORTIFICATIONS

LATE BRONZE AGE AND IRON AGE WALES

Hillforts, far and away the most impressive constructions of the prehistoric makers of Wales, were considered until recently to belong to the last few centuries of prehistory, and were believed to represent new defence methods necessitated by the use of iron weapons. Once again, radio-carbon dating has brought about a revolution, and it is now accepted that the earliest hillforts predate the Iron Age by several hundred years. The need for elaborate defences was probably the result of climatic change. In the centuries after about 1500 B.C., average temperatures fell by up to 5 degrees Fahrenheit, ushering in the Sub-Atlantic climatic period which has lasted until today. The change led to a shortening of the growing season, particularly at higher altitudes. Heavier rainfall brought about increased flooding in the lowlands; marshes multiplied and alluvial changes occurred in river valleys. Peat formation further undermined the viability of upland communities. Communities faced with a contraction in their agricultural land are likely to assert their territorial rights by building fortifications to defend them. The back-breaking toil involved in constructing the greater hillforts of Wales points to the existence of hierarchical societies having leaders with the power to force others to labour for them. The distribution of hillforts indicates a movement away from the higher altitudes to the margins of river valleys, locations convenient for the exploitation of fertile lowlands and for a continued but less intense use of the uplands.

There are almost six hundred hillforts in Wales, over a fifth of the British total. They vary greatly in design and size, and it may be indiscriminating to use the same term to denote all of them. A fifth of the surface area of Moel y

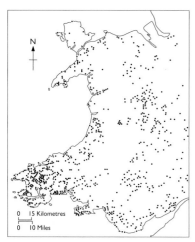

The distribution of Late Bronze Age and Iron Age hillforts in Wales and the borders.

Gaer on Halkyn Mountain has been stripped, revealing round huts dating from around 800 B.C.; some two hundred years later, a further group of round huts was built, together with a number of rectangular sheds — storage for winter fodder, perhaps. Less extensive excavations at others of the great hillforts of north-east Wales — Dinorben, Moel Hiraddug, Breiddin and Ffridd Faldwyn among them — have also yielded hut formations; indeed, some contained streets of houses laid out almost on town-planning principles, proof that the economy, in the last centuries of prehistory, in some parts of Wales at least, was capable of sustaining almost semi-urban communities.

The north-east has Wales's greatest concentration of large hillforts, but it is the north-west that contains one of the country's most remarkable prehistoric sites. That site is Tre'r Ceiri, near the summit of Yr Eifl, 14 miles (22.5km) south-west of Caernarfon. Its surrounding wall still stands up to 13 feet (4m) high, and within it are the ruins of over one hundred and fifty stone huts; some of them belong to the Roman period, although the settlement's origins are dated to about 200 B.C. Garn Goch, near Llangadog, is also a spectacular stone-walled settlement, but the prevalent pattern in south-west Wales is a multiplicity of fortlets; the area has over one hundred and fifty which are little more than an acre (0.5ha) in extent. Among the smaller hillforts of the south-west is Castell Henllys, east of Nevern, a well-fortified site containing recently reconstructed huts. The most dramatic of the fortlets are the cliff castles, simple structures consisting of a dyke and ditch across a promontory above the sea. Perhaps the most remarkable is at Flimston, west of St Govan's Head, where the fort is perilously poised above vertiginous cliffs.

The hillfort of Tre'r Ceiri, near the summit of Yr Eifl, on the Llŷn peninsula in north-west Wales. It is one of the country's most remarkable prehistoric sites, and a superb testament to the Iron Age makers of Wales (Crown Copyright: The Royal Commission on the Ancient and Historical Monuments of Wales).

Not all the settlement sites of Late Bronze Age and Iron Age Wales show up as hillfort enclosures. This 'cropmark' at Rhiwau near Llawhaden in Pembrokeshire shows the line of a small, strongly defended inner enclosure, perhaps occupied by a farmstead. The surrounding larger outer enclosure might represent the 'home fields' or a protected stockyard (Crown Copyright: The Royal Commission on the Ancient and Historical Monuments of Wales, 955010-58).

Several of the large hillforts have yielded evidence that iron was smelted and worked within their confines. The earliest iron object found in Wales is a sword dating from about 600 B.C., discovered in Llyn Fawr above the Rhondda. It may have been iron axes which allowed the great oaks of the valley bottoms to be felled. Pollen evidence from the Ystwyth valley indicates extensive clearing of the valley floor in the last centuries of prehistory. By then, over half the woodland canopy which had first come into existence in the Mesolithic period had ceased to exist. A folk memory of the clearances may be preserved in the early medieval Welsh story, *Culwch ac Olwen*: 'Do you see that great thicket out there?… I want it uprooted and burned on the ground down to cinders and ashes for manure; I want it ploughed and sown'.

Clearances meant creating fields, such as those that survive on the island of Skomer. There, the stone banks of Iron Age fields are immediately apparent, as are the lynchets — the steps formed when soil loosened by cultivation creeps downhill to pile against a field boundary. Banks and lynchets have also been found at Tŷ Mawr in Anglesey, at Hafoty Wernlas above Bontnewydd, at Caerau near Pantglas, and in many parts of Ardudwy, all in Gwynedd. But it is not wholly clear whether they are prehistoric. As on Skomer, the fields are very small. They probably reflect early ploughing methods — the use of the light ard which ripped the soil rather than turning the sod. The Welsh word *cyfair* means the area which can be ploughed in a day, and the so-called 'Celtic fields' may consist of a series of *cyfeiriau*.

The British Iron Age is conventionally considered to span the years from 600 B.C. to the first century of the Christian era. Yet to seek the terminal date is futile, for so useful has iron proved to be that the Iron Age has continued until today. The technology available to the people of the last centuries of prehistory would be the basis of life for many centuries to come, until indeed the material circumstances of the Welsh people were transformed in the last two hundred years. The makers of late prehistoric Wales were heirs to millennia of social, economic and technological development. And then came the Roman occupation, when Wales, for the first time, creeps into the historic record.

Llyn Fawr above the Rhondda was one of several lakes in Wales which appear to have been of sacred significance to the Iron Age makers of Wales. A hoard of iron and bronze objects was discovered in peat deposits at the site.

One of the earliest and rarest iron objects found in Britain is this sword fragment from the Llyn Fawr hoard of metalwork (National Museum & Gallery Cardiff).

Opposite: *The ditches of the Knave promontory fort on the south coast of the Gower peninsula show up particularly well in this aerial view (Crown Copyright: The Royal Commission on the Ancient and Historical Monuments of Wales).*

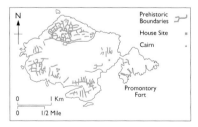

Above: *A sketch plan of the Iron Age field boundaries and house site on the Pembrokeshire island of Skomer.*

Left: *The size of the Skomer fields, seen here from the air, probably reflects the ploughing methods of the Iron Age makers of Wales (Crown Copyright: The Royal Commission on the Ancient and Historical Monuments of Wales, 935503-11).*

The face of 'Roman Winter' in Wales: A detail of the 'Seasons' mosaic excavated at the Roman town of Caerwent in 1901. Caerwent was the Roman Venta Silurum, *a provincial capital for the Silures, the late Celtic tribe of the region (Newport Museum and Art Gallery).*

WALES AND ROME

THE MAKING OF WALES FROM THE FIRST TO THE FOURTH CENTURIES

The Roman invasion of Britain was launched in A.D. 43. Wales came under attack in A.D. 48 when Ostorius Scapula and his forces reached the banks of the Dee. Sources show that north-east Wales was then inhabited by the Deceangli tribe; the north-west and much of central Wales was the home of the Ordovices, while the territory of the Cornovii extended to the central borderlands; the south-west was inhabited by the Demetae and the south-east by the Silures. The five known tribal groupings of Wales had probably been evolving over many centuries.

Within four years of the invasion, the south and east of Britain had become part of the empire, but the campaign to subjugate the inhabitants of Wales was not successfully concluded until A.D. 79. Most of the country had in fact been occupied by A.D. 60, but it was not immediately garrisoned. The collapse of the Roman plan for the full conquest of Wales at this time was the result of various factors beyond the immediate military situation. The subsequent delay of almost two decades meant the country had to be virtually reconquered in the late 70s. Temporary camps represent the initial impact made by the Romans upon the land of Wales. The first was probably at Rhun near Chirk, and its size indicates that a greater military force may have been used to subdue the Deceangli than is suggested by the historic record. Two impressive examples may be seen at Y Pigwn, east of Llandovery, where a 37-acre (15ha) camp is overlaid by another of 25 acres (10ha).

As the conquest proceeded, more permanent fortifications were constructed. The earliest — built about A.D. 60 — were at Clyro and Usk, but the most ambitious building project of the Romans in Wales began about A.D. 75 with the establishment of the legionary fortress at *Isca* (Caerleon). Over 50 acres (20ha) in extent, the fortress could accommodate up to 6,000 legionaries and in its north-west corner are the only Roman legionary barracks visible in Europe. Even more impressive is the amphitheatre just outside the walls. About two hundred years after its foundation, Caerleon was largely abandoned, but it proved inspiring even in ruin. In 1188 Gerald of Wales

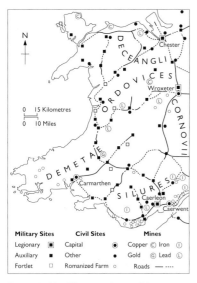

Roman Wales: The map shows all known military sites and the principal civilian settlements and Romanized farmsteads.

(d. 1223) wrote of it with awe; in 1405, the French forces supporting Owain Glyndŵr allegedly made a detour to visit the amphitheatre, long believed to be King Arthur's Round Table; Tennyson, when writing *The Idylls of the King*, stayed at Caerleon in order to absorb its atmosphere.

The establishment of the fortress was merely a part of the impact of the Roman empire upon the lower Usk valley. By A.D. 100 there was a civil settlement outside the walls, a port on the Usk and a *territorium* from which the fortress drew its raw materials. Legionaries were involved in transforming the landscape; a stone found at Goldcliff, 3 miles (5km) east of Uskmouth, records that the century of Statorus Maximus built a length of earthwork, part perhaps of the process of reclaiming and draining the levels of coastal Monmouthshire.

Caerleon was one of the two hubs of the Roman frontier in Wales; the legionary fortress at Chester was the other. They were linked to auxiliary forts, thirty-five of which have been discovered in Wales and its borderlands. Their impact upon the landscape can best be appreciated at *Segontium* (Caernarfon) or Y Gaer near Brecon. They were built to defend the empire against uprisings by the inhabitants of Wales, but by about A.D. 300 the main threat came from seaborne invaders, and the striking remains of the fortlet at Holyhead bear witness to the reaction of the Roman authorities.

The Roman legionary fortress of Isca *(Caerleon) seen from the air. Situated on the banks of the Usk, the fortress was designed to accommodate up to 6,000 legionaries. In the north-west corner of the fortress (foreground) are the only Roman legionary barracks visible in Europe.*

This inscribed stone from Goldcliff records that legionary soldiers were involved in building an earthwork on the Gwent (Monmouthshire) levels, perhaps part of a process of land reclamation (National Museum & Gallery Cardiff).

The Roman forts of Wales were linked in a tight grid with a system of metalled roads. This aerial photograph shows a stretch of the road known as 'Sarn Helen', near the upper reaches of the Swansea valley. The outline of the fort at Coelbren is visible to the upper right of the view (Committee for Aerial Photography, Cambridge University).

The Paulinus inscription at Caerwent provides confirmation of the civitas *status of the Roman town. Its community was self-governing, its officers meeting in an impressive 'town hall' within the centre of the Romanized settlement.*

Right: *The town walls at Caerwent were apparently built soon after A.D. 330 and continue to stand to an impressive height.*

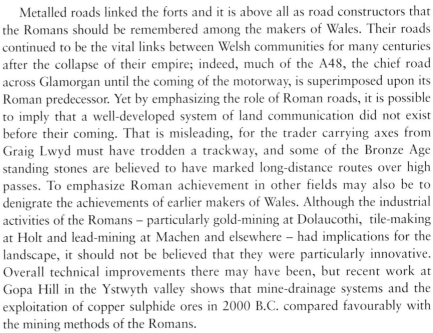

Metalled roads linked the forts and it is above all as road constructors that the Romans should be remembered among the makers of Wales. Their roads continued to be the vital links between Welsh communities for many centuries after the collapse of their empire; indeed, much of the A48, the chief road across Glamorgan until the coming of the motorway, is superimposed upon its Roman predecessor. Yet by emphasizing the role of Roman roads, it is possible to imply that a well-developed system of land communication did not exist before their coming. That is misleading, for the trader carrying axes from Graig Lwyd must have trodden a trackway, and some of the Bronze Age standing stones are believed to have marked long-distance routes over high passes. To emphasize Roman achievement in other fields may also be to denigrate the achievements of earlier makers of Wales. Although the industrial activities of the Romans – particularly gold-mining at Dolaucothi, tile-making at Holt and lead-mining at Machen and elsewhere – had implications for the landscape, it should not be believed that they were particularly innovative. Overall technical improvements there may have been, but recent work at Gopa Hill in the Ystwyth valley shows that mine-drainage systems and the exploitation of copper sulphide ores in 2000 B.C. compared favourably with the mining methods of the Romans.

A true innovation of the Romans in Wales was the town. The Romans established two *civitates* (provincial capitals) in Wales – for the Silures at *Venta Silurum* (Caerwent) and for the Demetae at *Moridunum* (Carmarthen). The evidence at Carmarthen is slight, but the *civitas* left a deep impression

upon the landscape, for *Moridunum's* boundaries can still be discerned in the plan of the modern town. At Caerwent the town's walls, built apparently after A.D. 330, still stand up to 20 feet (6m) high, although most of the dressed stone has been removed up to arm's reach. In its heyday, Caerwent had a population of perhaps some 3,000; despite its small size, it had all the appurtenances of a Roman city — a *forum-basilica* complex, bath-houses, a large hotel, at least three temples, shops, inns and a number of grand houses with mosaic floors, plastered walls and hypocaust heating. Over three-quarters of the later twentieth-century inhabitants of Wales are town-dwellers. In terms of the making of Wales, town-making is second only to field-making. It is a process which began at Caerwent.

The Roman planned city had its rural counterpart. This was the villa, the centre of an estate, a mansion Roman in style and comfort. The villas hitherto discovered in Wales are concentrated in southern Monmouthshire and the Vale of Glamorgan, where the fine example at Llantwit Major has been excavated. About two dozen sites in Wales are on occasion described as villas, but most of them are in fact Iron Age farms which have undergone varying degrees of Romanization. Whitton, near Bonvilston, is perhaps the best example. The villa owners were the pioneers of a more progressive agriculture; they introduced capitalist farming, a development assisted by the army's demand for grain. They encouraged heavier ploughing and contributed to the making of Wales by introducing new flora and fauna. It is possible that oats and apples were unknown in Wales before the conquest, and it is fairly certain that it was the Romans who introduced carrots, turnips, parsnips, leeks, cherries, vines, walnuts and sweet chestnuts. A less welcome newcomer was the black rat, the carrier of bubonic plague, a creature which must rank high among the unmakers of Wales.

The areas of Wales upon which the imprint of Rome can be clearly discerned constitute a small part of the country. Half a dozen partly-Romanized farms have been discovered in the south-west, but in mid and north Wales virtually no indigenous dwellings showing the influence of Roman building methods have been found. Numerous hut groups may be seen on the hills of Arfon and Llŷn; they are Iron Age in style but the occasional coins and pieces of pottery discovered in them are proof of some contact with the Roman world. Coins and pottery have also been found at the fine hut group at Din Lligwy in Anglesey and at Breiddin, near Montgomery, but Cors y Gedol in Merioneth, although occupied during the Roman occupation, has yielded virtually nothing of Roman provenance. It would thus appear that the inhabitants of the remoter parts of Wales had only slight and intermittent contact with things Roman. That would seem to be confirmed by the fact that Romanization was not thorough enough in Wales to ensure that the inhabitants abandoned their native language in favour of that of the conqueror. That is what happened in France, Italy and the Iberian peninsula, where, after the collapse of the empire, most of the inhabitants are found to be speaking forms of Latin which would evolve into French, Italian, Castilian, Catalan and Portuguese. The end of the empire left the inhabitants of Wales essentially speaking Brittonic, a language which would evolve into Welsh.

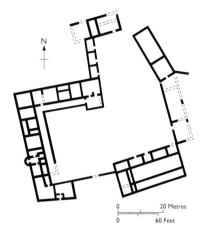

Villas or mansions in Roman style are known chiefly from south-east Wales. They served as centres of extensive rural estates. The best known example is that at Llantwit Major in the Vale of Glamorgan.

In the remoter parts of north and west Wales, it would appear that the native inhabitants had only slight and intermittent contact with things Roman. Here at Din Lligwy in Anglesey, although Roman pottery and coins have been found, the settlement and buildings remained essentially late Iron Age in style.

EARLY CHRISTIAN WALES

THE MAKING OF WALES FROM THE FIFTH TO THE ELEVENTH CENTURIES

The four or five centuries following the collapse of the Roman empire in the west was a vitally formative period for Wales and for the Welsh people. The country was to become geographically defined by the extent of the English conquests; its people were converted to Christianity by means which alas we do not fully understand (for we have no Welsh equivalent to the *Confessio* or autobiography of St Patrick); an early form of the Welsh language was developed and used (though rarely as yet) alongside the Latin of manuscripts and stone inscriptions. Still in touch, directly or indirectly with the Mediterranean and Gallic worlds, Wales was to evolve from a region on the mountainous fringe of a remote Roman province into a recognizable political and cultural entity. Whatever we choose to call the period — early Christian or early medieval (the older 'Dark Ages' going back to the period of the eighteenth-century Enlightenment has little to recommend it) — the period was crucial in the making of Wales.

The removal of Roman political authority at the end of the fourth century left power in the hands of local Welsh rulers or chieftains and their warbands, sometimes reinforced by new arrivals from Ireland and Scotland. By the sixth century, the Welsh cleric, Gildas, was castigating a series of kings in Wales and south-west England, many of whom were at least second generation rulers. Though Christians, like many medieval kings they showed scant respect for marriage vows or for the lives of those who stood in their way. The tombstone of one of the kings specifically named by Gildas — Vortipor of Dyfed — was found at Castell Dwyran in Carmarthenshire and is now in Carmarthen Museum. The stone reflects the diverse influences that went to make up early medieval Wales. It carries a Latin inscription (of sorts) giving Vortipor the Roman military title of 'Protector', with a parallel text in an early Irish script, as well as a Christian cross.

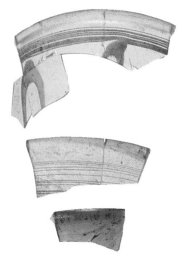

The seat of another chieftain or ruler of the period was excavated in the 1950s at Dinas Powys near Cardiff. His defended settlement was situated on the tip of a whale-backed limestone hill, with ditches cut into the bedrock and earth and rubble ramparts piled up behind them. The only evidence found of buildings revealed that they were of timber, and essentially unimpressive. But the ruler of Dinas Powys was able to provide his followers with feasts of beef and pork, no doubt tribute taken from the peasantry in return for his 'protection'. He and his retainers also enjoyed the contents of amphorae filled with olive oil and wine brought through Mediterranean and Atlantic trading networks from Syria, Asia Minor and the Aegean. At feasts the ruler was able to use tableware from what is now the western coast of Turkey, from Tunisia

The removal of Roman political authority at the end of the fourth century left power in early Christian Wales in the hands of local rulers or chieftains. The rock of Dinas Emrys in Snowdonia, the bluff seen at the centre of this view, appears to have been the seat of one of these rulers. Excavations have revealed evidence of a defended site occupied in the fifth and sixth centuries.

The importance of woodland management in early medieval Wales is reflected in the contents of Welsh Lawbooks — the law of Hywel. This illustration of trees represents coppicing (left) and lopping (right), and comes from a thirteenth-century manuscript (National Library of Wales, Peniarth Ms. 28, f. 22).

In the porch at Llanwnnws church, Cardiganshire, there is an early Christian inscribed stone. The church site may well be ancient, and now stands in splendid isolation. There was once perhaps a surrounding bond village which has now disappeared (Crown Copyright: The Royal Commission on the Ancient and Historical Monuments of Wales, 95-CS-0437).

and from western France, together with glass beakers again imported from France. His jeweller produced fine metalwork, including brooches decorated with enamel and millefiori glass. Recently, a cemetery of the same period, which has yielded sherds of similar amphorae, has been discovered on the nearby site of St Dochdwy's monastery at Llandough. This suggests that our anonymous ruler may well have been the patron and perhaps the founder of this early monastery, itself built on the site of a ruined Roman villa. Similar imported amphorae and glass are known from a number of other fortified seats of early Welsh chieftains, as at Hen Gastell in western Glamorgan, or at Degannwy on the mouth of the river Conwy — the traditional stronghold of Maelgwyn Gwynedd (d. 547), another of Gildas's rulers.

In general terms, all the sources suggest that Wales had a more impoverished society in the immediate post-Roman centuries than it had had in the Iron Age. Metal working continued, as at Dinas Powys, but there is no suggestion that masterpieces similar to those of the La Tène era in Europe were created. No attempt was made to construct anything remotely resembling the prehistoric hillforts. Dinas Powys, for example, is little more than 2.5 acres (1ha) in extent.

The decline in material culture in the fifth century is generally ascribed to the collapse of the economy following the downfall of the empire and to the ravages caused by barbarian attacks. There is some evidence of other adversities, including plague epidemics and a deterioration in the climate. Yet, as pollen studies do not suggest a massive return of woodland, the inhabitants of early Christian Wales were at least capable of maintaining the open spaces won by their predecessors over the millennia. Domesday Book, which provides details of the settlement pattern in parts of the Welsh borderland in 1086, implies that only 16 per cent of eastern Flintshire consisted of forested land.

Some nineteenth-century historians maintained that early Christian Wales was inhabited by semi-nomadic people and known sites of permanent settlement belonging to the era are therefore scarce because they hardly existed. Topographical studies and analysis of the documentary evidence — in particular the earliest substrata of the Welsh Lawbooks — have led to a different conclusion. Society did have a limited nomadic element, for in late spring a proportion of the population moved with their flocks and herds from the *hendref* (the winter home) to the *hafod* (the summer home). The shape of the *cantrefi* — in Glamorgan, for example — indicates the essential unity of highland and lowland. A society which practises transhumance is not necessarily nomadic, for it can have settled roots in the lowlands. A nomadic society does not grow crops. The querns (hand-mills) found at sites such as Dinas Powys, Dinas Emrys and Dinorben prove that grain was an integral part of the diet, and arable fields cultivated around A.D. 600 have been discovered at Pant y Saer in Anglesey.

The Welsh countryside today is a landscape of dispersed settlement, but that may not always have been the case. The Lawbooks discuss the responsibility of a householder if fire spreads from his house to that of a neighbour, an indication of the existence of nucleated settlements. It is now believed that the majority of the inhabitants of Wales in the immediate post-Roman centuries were *taeogion* — unfree cultivators of the soil — and that the free population — the *bonheddwyr* (those with *bon* or honourable ancestry) — would not constitute a significant proportion of the population for centuries to come. The *taeogion* dwelt in *taeogdrefi* (bond villages), where they worked under the direction of the *maer* to supply food rents for their masters. There was a *maerdref* within half a mile (0.8km) of the Dinorben hillfort. This suggests that medieval patterns had roots going back to the Iron Age, and it has been argued that continuity in settlement is far greater than most historians have been prepared to admit.

From the sixth or seventh centuries, the Welsh Church became predominantly monastic, though it is important to remember that it was an integral part of western Christendom. The old term 'Celtic Church' is now little used, since it can imply that the Welsh Church was in some way separate from the wider Christian faith. Some of the older churches are believed to have been built in the centre of *taeogdrefi*. A note in the margin of the *Book of Teilo*, written in about 825, mentions Gwaun Henllan (the meadow of the old church). The reference is to the parish church of Llandybie; the church of St Tybie is located at the centre of a substantial village, but many of the ancient church sites of Wales now stand in splendid isolation, indicative, probably, of the decay and disappearance of the bond villages which once surrounded them.

The memory of many of the monastic founders is preserved in churches such as Llantwit Major (Llanilltud Fawr), the monastery of St Illtud, or Llancarfan where St Cadog founded a monastery. In each case, the saint presided over a *clas* (a Celtic monastic community). In northern Powys, Tysilio similarly presided over the *clas* at Meifod; the present-day 10-acre (4ha) Meifod churchyard occupies the site of the *clas*, which served as the necropolis of the kings of Powys. Other churchyards — Llandeilo Fawr, Llanynys, Clynnog Fawr, Llangurig and Glascwm — also represent the sites of ancient *clasau*. Many of these sites still retain sculptured crosses of the period, though sadly, the pre-Norman church buildings of Wales have left no readily detectable trace. But the location of churches and monasteries played a part in determining settlement patterns, and places of Christian worship continue to be a dominating feature of the townscape and the countryside.

The desire of the early Church to commemorate its leaders and saints gave Wales its most widespread form of place-name. The word *llan* means an enclosure; in place-names it usually denotes a sanctified burial ground and centuries may have passed before a church was built within it. Parishes bearing *llan* names cover well over half the surface area of Wales; they have their origin in the early Christian era and must be accounted one of the country's most basic building-blocks.

However, the chief tangible remains of early Christian Wales are its inscribed and decorated stones. In all, there are about 450 of them dating from the fifth to the eleventh centuries. The earliest group of these stones, about 140 examples in all, demonstrates clear links with both Ireland and the western shores of mainland Europe. These early memorial stones or

From the sixth or seventh centuries, the Welsh Church became predominantly monastic. The parish church at Llantwit Major (Llanilltud Fawr) preserves the memory of the important monastery of St Illtud (Robert Williams).

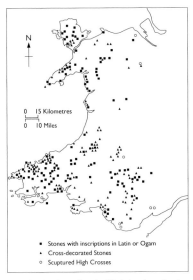

- ■ Stones with inscriptions in Latin or Ogam
- ▲ Cross-decorated Stones
- ○ Sculptured High Crosses

The distribution of early Christian inscribed and decorated stones in Wales.

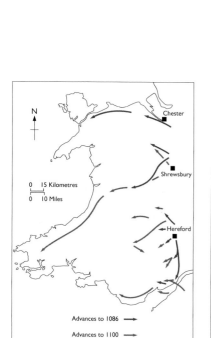

For three hundred years after the Norman Conquest, castle-building was to be the most obtrusive activity of the makers of Wales. As this scene from the Bayeux Tapestry illustrates, the process began as part of the conquest itself. The castle was the key to Norman advance in Wales.

Early Norman aggression in Wales took the form of attack on several fronts from bases on the Welsh border, and from across the Severn estuary.

THE IMPACT OF THE NORMANS

THE MAKING OF WALES 1070–1170

In the making of Wales, the contribution of the Normans was among the most enduring. The aggressive impulses of the Anglo-Saxons had ebbed away by the time they reached the Welsh uplands. Those of the Normans did not, for they, perhaps more than any other of the peoples of medieval Europe, were colonists by instinct and inheritance.

The Old English Kingdom had attained a remarkable degree of consolidation, and following his victory at Hastings in 1066, King William I (1066–87) won such mastery over it that, within twenty years of his accession, he was able to order the compilation of Domesday Book, the foundation document of English landscape studies. Power in Wales was far more decentralized, and destroying the power of the native Welsh dynasties proved a protracted and piecemeal business. Initiated by border lords, but increasingly undertaken by the Norman kings and their Angevin successors, the process took over two hundred years.

The long conflict left a profound impress upon the landscape of Wales. The key to Norman advance in Wales was the castle. The earlier a region was invaded, the greater the number of castles it contains; thus the old county of Glamorgan has thirty stone castles, compared with one in Anglesey. Norman aggression took the form of a four-pronged attack — upon Gwent from Hereford, upon Powys and Deheubarth from Shrewsbury, upon Gwynedd from Chester and upon Glamorgan from across the Severn estuary — and in each case the aggressors sought to convert victory into permanent domination through the construction of castles.

William fitz Osbern (d. 1071) and his son Roger, during their brief tenure of the earldom of Hereford (1067–75), proved to be vigorous castle-builders. Among their constructions were those at Monmouth and Chepstow, the keys to their conquest of the kingdom of Gwent. Most of the early Norman castles

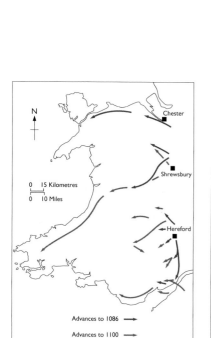

Advances to 1086 ⟶

Advances to 1100 ⟶

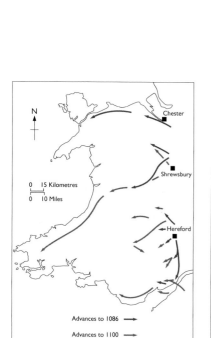

15 Kilometres

10 Miles

majority of the inhabitants of Wales in the immediate post-Roman centuries were *taeogion* — unfree cultivators of the soil — and that the free population — the *bonheddwyr* (those with *bon* or honourable ancestry) — would not constitute a significant proportion of the population for centuries to come. The *taeogion* dwelt in *taeogdrefi* (bond villages), where they worked under the direction of the *maer* to supply food rents for their masters. There was a *maerdref* within half a mile (0.8km) of the Dinorben hillfort. This suggests that medieval patterns had roots going back to the Iron Age, and it has been argued that continuity in settlement is far greater than most historians have been prepared to admit.

From the sixth or seventh centuries, the Welsh Church became predominantly monastic, though it is important to remember that it was an integral part of western Christendom. The old term 'Celtic Church' is now little used, since it can imply that the Welsh Church was in some way separate from the wider Christian faith. Some of the older churches are believed to have been built in the centre of *taeogdrefi*. A note in the margin of the *Book of Teilo*, written in about 825, mentions Gwaun Henllan (the meadow of the old church). The reference is to the parish church of Llandybie; the church of St Tybie is located at the centre of a substantial village, but many of the ancient church sites of Wales now stand in splendid isolation, indicative, probably, of the decay and disappearance of the bond villages which once surrounded them.

The memory of many of the monastic founders is preserved in churches such as Llantwit Major (Llanilltud Fawr), the monastery of St Illtud, or Llancarfan where St Cadog founded a monastery. In each case, the saint presided over a *clas* (a Celtic monastic community). In northern Powys, Tysilio similarly presided over the *clas* at Meifod; the present-day 10-acre (4ha) Meifod churchyard occupies the site of the *clas*, which served as the necropolis of the kings of Powys. Other churchyards — Llandeilo Fawr, Llanynys, Clynnog Fawr, Llangurig and Glascwm — also represent the sites of ancient *clasau*. Many of these sites still retain sculptured crosses of the period, though sadly, the pre-Norman church buildings of Wales have left no readily detectable trace. But the location of churches and monasteries played a part in determining settlement patterns, and places of Christian worship continue to be a dominating feature of the townscape and the countryside.

The desire of the early Church to commemorate its leaders and saints gave Wales its most widespread form of place-name. The word *llan* means an enclosure; in place-names it usually denotes a sanctified burial ground and centuries may have passed before a church was built within it. Parishes bearing *llan* names cover well over half the surface area of Wales; they have their origin in the early Christian era and must be accounted one of the country's most basic building-blocks.

However, the chief tangible remains of early Christian Wales are its inscribed and decorated stones. In all, there are about 450 of them dating from the fifth to the eleventh centuries. The earliest group of these stones, about 140 examples in all, demonstrates clear links with both Ireland and the western shores of mainland Europe. These early memorial stones or

From the sixth or seventh centuries, the Welsh Church became predominantly monastic. The parish church at Llantwit Major (Llanilltud Fawr) preserves the memory of the important monastery of St Illtud (Robert Williams).

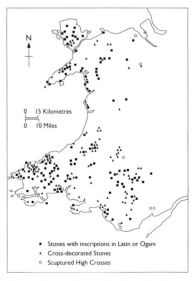

The distribution of early Christian inscribed and decorated stones in Wales.

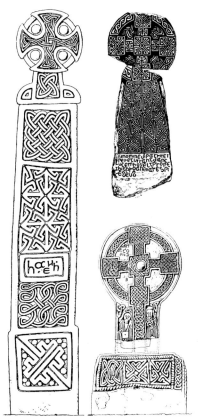

Illustrations of three of the finest early Christian monuments in Wales: To the left is the Carew cross, commemorating King Maredudd of Deheubarth (d. 1035); the top right example is the superb disc-headed slab at Llantwit Major, a late ninth-century memorial to King Rhys put up by his son Hywel ap Rhys; and to the bottom right is the late ninth- or early tenth-century Cynfelyn stone, the largest and most elaborate of the Welsh disc-headed slabs.

tombstones are found mostly in west Wales. Some carry inscriptions in old Irish, written in an Irish alphabet of dots and dashes (rather like the Morse Code) known as ogam script. One stone, from Penmachno in Gwynedd, claims to have been put up in the time of the Roman consul Justinus, whose consulship in A.D. 540 was used in the Lyon area of France as the base line for a dating system. Other stones carry the Latin Filius, 'son of', important in a tribal society where genealogy and ancestry were of paramount importance. Later, these Latin inscriptions were replaced by stones bearing simple crosses, with no inscriptions, and in time the use of sculpture for crosses and memorial stones spread into Wales from adjacent parts of England and Ireland.

The concentrations of stones at major Christian centres such as Llantwit Major, St Davids, Margam and Llanbadarn Fawr suggest that most of them were erected under the auspices of the *clasau*; like the *llan* names, they primarily represent the desire to commemorate the founders and the sustainers of the Christianity of Wales. But as with the Vortipor stone, some examples are memorials to secular figures. There is another, for instance, at Llangadwaladr Church in Anglesey, where the tombstone commemorates King Cadfan of Gwynedd, who died in about 625. But the fullest inscription is that on the monument erected near Llangollen in memory of King Eliseg of Powys, who died in about 760. Llantwit Major, which was probably the necropolis of the royal house of Glamorgan, has several memorials to secular rulers, including one to King Rhys, who died in 860. The crosses at Nevern, Penally and Carew represent the apogee of the art of the early Welsh stone-carvers; that at Carew commemorates King Maredudd of Deheubarth, who died in 1035.

While inscribed stones offer evidence of the whereabouts of Welsh rulers after death, little has come to light concerning their whereabouts when they were alive. Of the major kingdoms of early medieval Wales, tradition maintains that the ancestral seat of the dynasty of Gwynedd was at Aberffraw, of Powys at Mathrafal and of Deheubarth at Dinefwr. Excavations at Aberffraw and Mathrafal have as yet proved disappointing, and the original Dinefwr seat may lie beneath the later stone castle. Thus virtually nothing can be said about the residences of rulers such as Rhodri Mawr (d. 877), Hywel Dda (d. 950) and Maredudd ab Owain (d. 999). Work on the probable seat of the kings of Brycheiniog — the crannog at Llangorse Lake — is proving promising. The crannog is artificial and was created by piling rubbish upon a timber and wattle framed raft located 130 feet (40m) from the lake's northern shore, where the water is only some 4 feet (1.2m) deep. Tree-ring studies suggest that considerable work was undertaken on the site between about 860 and 910. The crannog is the only one as yet discovered in Wales and is similar to many of those in Ireland. Thus it seems likely that links between Ireland and Brycheiniog, for which there is considerable evidence from the fifth and sixth centuries, were still significant four hundred years later.

Although landscape evidence relating to the activities of the early rulers of Wales is slight, other evidence indicates that the dynasties to which they belonged were remarkably stable and powerful enough to ensure that the Vikings, who occupied large parts of Ireland, Scotland and England, only succeeded in establishing minor colonies in Wales. Undoubtedly the chief visible tribute to the power of the Welsh rulers is Offa's Dyke, the most impressive monument constructed in Britain in the second half of the first Christian millennium. The dyke, built under the aegis of Offa, king of Mercia from 757 to 796, was an admission that the English were unlikely to be able to extend their power to Wales. Offa's intention was to provide Mercia with a well-defined boundary from Prestatyn to Chepstow, a distance of 150 miles (240km). Yet the dyke is not unbroken; there is a gap at its northern end, natural barriers such as rivers were used on occasion, and in the south the dyke was constructed only in short stretches where English settlement had penetrated the natural forest of the region. A total of 80 miles (130km) of dyke was built.

In the planning of the dyke, there seems to have been a degree of consultation with the rulers of Powys and Gwent, for on occasion its alignment was advantageous to the Welsh rulers rather than to Mercia. At its most impressive, Offa's Dyke is up to 20 feet (6m) high, with a ditch on both its western and eastern sides. It can be seen at its best in three areas: near Chirk Castle, where its course coincides with the present border between Wales and England; east of Montgomery, where that occurs again, and around Knighton, where there is an admirable dyke interpretation centre.

When constructed, Offa's Dyke broadly denoted a racial frontier that had been in existence for at least a century. The frontier did not prove to be stable. Gruffudd ap Llywelyn (d. 1063), the only ruler to win authority over the whole of Wales, won back extensive territories, particularly in the north-east. Yet, during his reign, other forces were gathering strength. In 1053, Ralf, the Norman nephew of the English king, Edward the Confessor (1042–66), became a powerful figure in Herefordshire. He built castles in the county, an activity hitherto unknown in Anglo-Saxon England. One of them was at Womaston, south of Presteigne, less than 120 yards (107m) west of the present Wales—England border; it was to prove a fateful act.

Assuming that all the sections which bear his name were raised under the aegis of Offa of Mercia, the king was responsible for a total of 80 miles (130km) of dyke. This section is near Chirk Castle on the northern border. The dyke played an important part in shaping the perception of the extent and identity of Wales (Crown Copyright: The Royal Commission on the Ancient and Historical Monuments of Wales).

The artificial island or crannog in Llangorse Lake, Powys, was the probable seat of the kings of Brycheiniog around A.D. 900.

For three hundred years after the Norman Conquest, castle-building was to be the most obtrusive activity of the makers of Wales. As this scene from the Bayeux Tapestry illustrates, the process began as part of the conquest itself. The castle was the key to Norman advance in Wales.

THE IMPACT OF THE NORMANS

THE MAKING OF WALES 1070–1170

In the making of Wales, the contribution of the Normans was among the most enduring. The aggressive impulses of the Anglo-Saxons had ebbed away by the time they reached the Welsh uplands. Those of the Normans did not, for they, perhaps more than any other of the peoples of medieval Europe, were colonists by instinct and inheritance.

The Old English Kingdom had attained a remarkable degree of consolidation, and following his victory at Hastings in 1066, King William I (1066–87) won such mastery over it that, within twenty years of his accession, he was able to order the compilation of Domesday Book, the foundation document of English landscape studies. Power in Wales was far more decentralized, and destroying the power of the native Welsh dynasties proved a protracted and piecemeal business. Initiated by border lords, but increasingly undertaken by the Norman kings and their Angevin successors, the process took over two hundred years.

The long conflict left a profound impress upon the landscape of Wales. The key to Norman advance in Wales was the castle. The earlier a region was invaded, the greater the number of castles it contains; thus the old county of Glamorgan has thirty stone castles, compared with one in Anglesey. Norman aggression took the form of a four-pronged attack — upon Gwent from Hereford, upon Powys and Deheubarth from Shrewsbury, upon Gwynedd from Chester and upon Glamorgan from across the Severn estuary — and in each case the aggressors sought to convert victory into permanent domination through the construction of castles.

William fitz Osbern (d. 1071) and his son Roger, during their brief tenure of the earldom of Hereford (1067–75), proved to be vigorous castle-builders. Among their constructions were those at Monmouth and Chepstow, the keys to their conquest of the kingdom of Gwent. Most of the early Norman castles

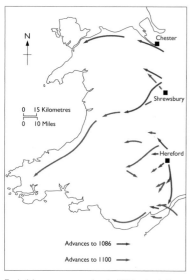

Early Norman aggression in Wales took the form of attack on several fronts from bases on the Welsh border, and from across the Severn estuary.

By 1075, the narrow ridge above the Wye at Chepstow had been crowned by a stone hall-keep, Britain's earliest datable secular stone building. From this castle stronghold, advances were made into the former Welsh kingdom of Gwent.

Most of the early Norman castles in Wales were of the motte-and-bailey variety. The motte was a great earthen mound, topped with a tower of wood. It was surrounded by a ditch, with an adjoining fortified bailey. Painscastle in Powys is a particularly impressive example (Crown Copyright: The Royal Commission on the Ancient and Historical Monuments of Wales).

The Normans also employed the ringwork castle — a substantial bank and surrounding ditch enclosing a circular area. Although undocumented, Caerau, Ely, near Cardiff, has the appearance of a classic Norman ringwork (Crown Copyright: The Royal Commission on the Ancient and Historical Monuments of Wales).

were of the motte-and-bailey variety, although the favoured structure in the Vale of Glamorgan and around Pembroke, for example, was the ringwork. The latter consisted of a bank and ditch enclosing a circular area, while the former was an earthen mound (the motte) surrounded by a ditch and with an adjoining fortified bailey. The motte, which could be up to 50 feet (15m) in height, was intended to overawe and to provide permanent evidence of the might of the conqueror. It was topped by a tower built of wood, a material chosen partly because a freshly raised mound cannot bear the weight of masonry and partly because a timber structure can be erected cheaply and rapidly — a motte-and-bailey castle could be completed in as little as eight days. However, one of the castles of the Norman invaders of Wales was a stone construction virtually from its inception. By 1075, the narrow ridge above the Wye at Chepstow had been crowned, not by a tower, but by a hall-keep, medieval Britain's earliest datable secular stone building. Its style is very similar to broadly contemporary work in Normandy, such as the hall-keep at Falaise, the birthplace of William the Conqueror.

Initially it seemed as if the invasion would rapidly bring the whole of Wales under the control of the Normans. Even Gwynedd, protected by the ramparts of Snowdonia, seemed ripe for conquest, for the Normans swept across it and constructed an impressive motte at Aberlleiniog, at the south-eastern extremity of Anglesey. However, the invaders had overreached themselves, for as a result of the Welsh risings of the 1090s, their domination in the north came to be restricted to a narrow strip along the estuary of the Dee. In mid Wales their losses were even more striking, for there the Welsh successes culminated in 1095 with the capture of Old Montgomery Castle (Hen Domen), the launching pad of the invasion of Powys. The rising was almost as successful in the south-west, where the Normans were driven from all their strongholds

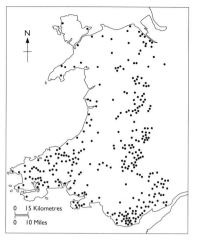

The distribution of earthwork castles (mottes and ringworks) in Wales.

with the significant exception of their castle at Pembroke. Parts of the south-east were also convulsed with revolt, but there the insurgents failed to capture the castles.

The success of the Welsh uprising, although not complete, forced the Normans to conclude that, unless they devoted disproportionate resources to the subjection of Wales, they would have to be content to permit Welsh rulers to hold sway over much of the country. Thus the twelfth century saw the emergence of three zones in Wales. The north-eastern borderlands around Hawarden and Mold, the vicinities of Montgomery and Radnor, the lower Wye and Usk valleys, the Vale of Glamorgan, Gower, the area south of Carmarthen and southern Dyfed were all firmly under Anglo-Norman domination. Gwynedd, Powys, Ceredigion and Ystrad Tywi (roughly the later Carmarthenshire) continued under Welsh dynasties. In between lay the upper Wye, upland Brecon, Gwent and Glamorgan and northern Dyfed, areas over which the Anglo-Normans exercised spasmodic control.

The regions firmly under Anglo-Norman control later became known as *Marchia Wallie* (the March of Wales); those under Welsh rule were *Pura Wallia*, while the intermediate areas were part sometimes of the one *Wallia* and sometimes of the other. The division had implications for the making of Wales. Although the rulers of *Pura Wallia* began to build castles — Trallwng (Welshpool), near the later Powis Castle, built by Cadwgan ap Bleddyn by 1111, was perhaps the earliest of them — *Marchia Wallie* was the true domain of the castle, at least in the century following the launching of the Norman invasions. Little now remains of the fortified buildings erected in Wales during that century. The vast majority of the four hundred and more castles built in Wales and its borders never consisted of anything more than wooden structures. As their timber has long rotted away, they feature on the landscape as earthworks rather than as buildings. A minority — those which developed administrative and domestic roles as well as a long-term military function — were rebuilt in stone. Thus, a stone shell keep had taken the place of the wooden tower at Cardiff, at least by 1158, when it was attacked by Ifor Bach; Gerald of Wales (born in 1145) spent his boyhood within the stone walls of

The earliest documentary reference to Manorbier Castle in Pembrokeshire dates from 1146. The earliest masonry structures at the site could belong to this period, though the curtain walls probably date to about 1230.

Manorbier Castle and Rhys ap Gruffudd (d. 1197) — the Lord Rhys — had erected a castle of 'masonry and mortar' at Cardigan by 1174. Little of the building work which would have been familiar to Ifor Bach, Gerald and Rhys is now visible, for in late twelfth- and thirteenth-century Wales, strategically placed castles were subjected to vast programmes of rebuilding.

As well as being the domain of the castle, *Marchia Wallie* was also the first region of Wales to experience the rebirth of the town. There is growing evidence that there was an urban settlement at Monmouth when it was part of the Welsh kingdom of Gwent, and the Anglo-Saxons established the *burh* of Clwydmouth (*Cledemutha*) at Rhuddlan in about 921. The extensive planting of towns in Wales did not occur, however, until the coming of the Normans. By 1170, Wales had about fifty settlements with at least some pretensions to urban status, the great majority of them in the regions under secure Anglo-Norman control. Yet by then, towns were not unknown in *Pura Wallia*. The borough of Cardigan, which came into the possession of Lord Rhys of Deheubarth in 1165, was fostered by its new ruler, and in Gwynedd and Powys quasi-urban communities were coming into existence. The towns of late eleventh- and twelfth-century Wales were very small compared with what they would be in the heyday of urban settlement in the late thirteenth century. In 1086 Rhuddlan had eighteen burgesses, and in the 1090s the burgesses of Brecon lived, not in a settlement distinct from the castle, but in the outer bailey of the castle itself.

The towns, like the castles, were not immediately protected by masonry; Carmarthen, in the 1230s, was perhaps the first borough in Wales to be provided with stone walls. Yet materials other than stone — palisades, banks and ditches — could provide elaborate defences. Norman Rhuddlan was surrounded by extensive earthworks, enclosing a total of 35 acres (14ha). The invaders were aware of the vulnerability of their urban plantations in Wales. At the height of medieval town-building, 86 per cent of the towns of Wales had defences, compared with 38 per cent in England, and in Wales, unlike in most of England, burgesses were obliged to undertake military service. The boroughs created in Wales in the late thirteenth century had a regular plan, but planned towns were an aberration rather than the norm. Indeed, most of the towns of early twelfth-century Wales probably consisted of little more than a single street leading from the town gate to the castle.

The primary role of the borough was to serve the needs of the castle garrison. Yet the greater the success of the invaders, the less the garrison was needed, and towns which did not attain a role beyond the military were doomed to failure. The town's secondary, and eventually its primary role was to serve as a centre of specialization and exchange in what was a rural, largely subsistence economy. In later Monmouthshire, a network of towns came into existence, each serving a hinterland about 6 miles (10km) in radius. Thus Usk, 9 miles (14km) from Trelleck, 10 miles (16km) from Monmouth and from Abergavenny, 13 miles (21km) from Newport and 14 miles (22km) from Chepstow, could sustain some semblance of urban life. A similar pattern emerged in the Vale of Glamorgan and in the lordship of Pembroke, and ultimately in other parts of Wales also.

The great Norman motte at Rhuddlan was established on the banks of the river Clwyd in 1073. An infant borough grew up around the stronghold, with eighteen burgesses or townsmen recorded in 1086.

The Norman castle at Pembroke was established in 1093 by Earl Roger of Shrewsbury (d. 1094). A town began to emerge in the shadow of the stronghold, and this was given a borough charter by King Henry I in 1100. The shape of the town was determined by the peninsula on which it stood. The town walls look very early and could date to the first years of the thirteenth century (Crown Copyright: The Royal Commission on the Ancient and Historical Monuments of Wales, 93-CS-0246).

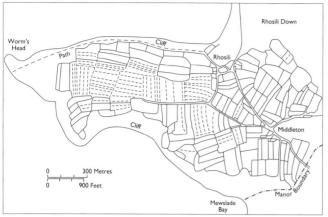

Throughout the Norman period, Wales remained an overwhelmingly rural country. From the early 1100s, the Gower peninsula, for example, became a patchwork of knights' fees, with nucleated villages at the centre of manorial open fields. At Rhossili, on the south-west corner of the peninsula, the remains of an open field system — known locally as 'the Vile' — can still be seen. As the aerial photograph reveals, the strip pattern of fields remains quite distinct. The map, based on an original of 1780, shows the 'fossilized' medieval layout, with the fields still communally occupied (Photograph, Crown Copyright: The Royal Commission on the Ancient and Historical Monuments of Wales, 95-CS-1205).

In the twelfth century, town-dwellers hardly constituted 5 per cent of the population. Although the innovative forces represented by the boroughs were of great significance, *Marchia Wallie*, and even more so *Pura Wallia*, were overwhelmingly rural. As with castles and boroughs, so also with the countryside, the Normans left an enduring mark. Along with the castle, the key to the success of their incursions was the knight, a mounted warrior who gave allegiance and military service to his lord in return for material support, usually in the form of an estate. The lands firmly under Anglo-Norman control became a patchwork of knights' fees, a development which went far to obliterate earlier territorial divisions. The power of the incomers was further strengthened by encouraging substantial colonization of their newly won lands by peasants — from England in the main, but also from Flanders and France. The colonists stamped their traditions on the land. The Devonshire customary acre was imported into the Gower peninsula and the Flemings brought their skills as sheep-rearers to the region around Haverfordwest. Where colonists were numerous, Welsh place-names gave way to those of the newcomers. Wales has 350 early examples of place-names with the suffix -ton, of which 155 are in Pembrokeshire, 74 in Glamorgan, 35 in Monmouthshire and 25 in Flintshire. Many of the settlers were villeins — unfree tenants working the manorial land for their lord. They brought with them the arable traditions of

In the rich areas of Wales which were firmly under Anglo-Norman control, the arable traditions of the English lowlands became commonplace. Crop-raising was encouraged by the demands of a growing population, and corn-mills proliferated. The annual round of the corn harvest was perhaps little different from the scene depicted in this fourteenth-century manuscript (The British Library, Additional Ms. 42130, f. 172v).

the English lowlands, and crop-raising was further encouraged by the demands of an increasing population, a development aided by the milder climate of the century or so after 1080. Thus, corn-mills proliferated; almost all of them were the lord's property, a factor which greatly contributed to his power over his peasantry.

The area colonized under the Normans constituted but a small part of the country. Welsh patterns of landholding continued in existence, even in lowland Gwent, the Vale of Glamorgan and the Gower peninsula. They were overwhelmingly dominant in upland Gwent and Glamorgan and were, in the twelfth century, wholly unchallenged in Gwynedd, Ceredigion and most of Powys and Ystrad Tywi.

In native Wales, the older local unit, the *cantref*, was giving way to the smaller unit, the *cwmwd* (the commote). Each had a *llys* or court, one of a number of seats of the ruler. Several of these survive in place-names — Llysfasi, the *llys* of the commote of Llannerch in Dyffryn Clwyd, for example — but archaeological evidence is sparse as yet, although interesting work has been done at Rhosyr in Anglesey. The *llysoedd* of rulers such as Gruffudd ap Cynan (d. 1137) of Gwynedd probably consisted of an enclosure containing a group of timber buildings, the most prominent of which was the *neuadd* (the hall), where the court officials so meticulously described in the Welsh Lawbooks served their ruler and where he entertained his nobility with feasting, music and the declamations of his poets.

Near the *llys* dwelt the ruler's hereditary servile class, the *taeogion*, and they worked their strips of land under the close supervision of their masters. The land of the free population, the *bonheddwyr*, also tended to become fragmented, for each son of a freeman had an equal right to the property of his father. Writing in 1603, George Owen of Henllys described the consequences of gavelkind (the equal division of land among sons): 'The whole countrie was brought into smale peeces of ground and intermingled upp and downe with another, so as in every five or sixe acres you shall have ten or twelve owners'.

In the late eleventh century, the whole pattern of life in Wales was on the verge of profound transformation. That was partly because of the Norman incursions. While they led to new kinds of settlement in places such as Pembroke and the Vale of Glamorgan, they also resulted in much dislocation in those regions which swung back and forth between Anglo-Norman and Welsh control. Other regions, Gwynedd in particular, enjoyed greater stability, especially under the rule of Gruffudd ap Cynan and his son, Owain Gwynedd (d. 1170), and Gruffudd's biographer described the extensive establishment of orchards and gardens. Increasing prosperity could undermine age-old practices, as could the embryonic money economy which came with the growth of towns. Above all, the population increased; indeed Wales by 1300 may have had as many as three times the number of inhabitants it had had in 1070.

In the transformation of Wales, a powerful role was played by the Church. The Norman incursions coincided with the surge for reform which swept through the western Church in the late eleventh century. The Normans were

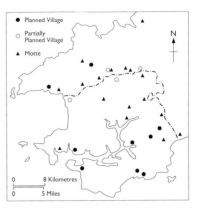

There is good evidence to suggest that a number of villages in south Wales were deliberately planted by the Norman conquerors. This map shows the extent of such planned villages in Pembrokeshire, with the loose frontier between Anglo-Norman and Welsh areas marked (After Jonathan Kissock).

Templeton in Pembrokeshire was almost certainly a planned village planted by the Norman conquerors. Elements of its regular form can still be seen (Crown Copyright: The Royal Commission on the Ancient and Historical Monuments of Wales, 90-CS-565).

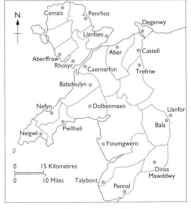

North-west Wales, showing the commote boundaries. Each local division had a *llys* or court, one of a number of seats of the ruler.

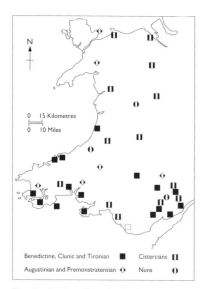

The distribution of medieval religious houses in Wales.

Above: *The Norman conquerors of Wales brought with them the brand of Latin monasticism with which they were familiar: Benedictine priories were established, often in the new boroughs and in the shadow of the invaders' castles. Ewenny was an exception, built as it was away from both town and castle. However, like all medieval religious houses, the church and principal monastic buildings were surrounded by a substantial precinct.*

Right: *The south transept in the priory church at Ewenny reveals the quality of the very finest Romanesque architecture in Anglo-Norman Wales.*

godly in their way, faithful to the papacy which had blessed their venture in England. To enthusiastic reformers, the distinctive features of the Welsh Church — the product of centuries of isolation — were abhorrent. The *clas* churches had married abbots and hereditary offices; the bishops were neither members of a defined hierarchy nor pastors of clearly demarcated dioceses; the building of great stone churches, work already afoot in Normandy and England, had not begun; the country lacked monasteries obedient to the *Rule of Saint Benedict*, the most powerful of the influences giving unity to Latin Europe.

By 1170, Norman power and influence had gone far to correct these perceived deficiencies, and as a result monuments had been created and territorial units had been established which were among the most important contributions to the making of Wales. Up to a dozen Benedictine priories were established. Chepstow, the earliest, founded by William fitz Osbern in 1071, had massive piers characteristic of Romanesque at its most monumental. Ewenny, founded by the de Londres family, lords of Ogwr, in 1116–41, is perhaps the finest example of Romanesque architecture in Wales. It is the only Benedictine priory in Wales not built within or adjoining a Norman borough, and the fortress-like architecture seems to echo Norman insecurity. It was a cell of the great Benedictine abbey of Gloucester, and Gloucester's abbot advised the prior of Ewenny to 'strengthen the locks of your doors and surround your house with a good ditch and an impregnable wall', proof of the suspicion of the Welsh harboured by the promoters of the first phase of Latin monasticism in Wales.

The earliest Norman bishop of St Davids was appointed in 1115. The present cathedral church was commenced under Bishop Peter de Leia (1176–98), with the nave another superb example of Anglo-Norman Romanesque architecture.

All the Benedictine houses of Wales were cells of abbeys outside Wales. In addition, the revenues of the *clas* churches, at least in southern Wales, were bestowed upon churches elsewhere. A similar fate befell many Welsh parish churches, for the Normans carried out a massive disendowment of the Church in Wales. They also demoted native Welsh saints, with St Tathan giving way to St Stephen at Caerwent, St Teilo yielding precedence to St Peter at Llandaff and St David losing some pre-eminence to St Andrew at St Davids.

Yet there were more constructive aspects to the activities of the Normans. The Benedictine priories are not the only buildings in Wales offering examples of Romanesque architecture. At Llandaff, the work of the diocese's first Norman bishop, Urban (1107–34), survives in the fine arch between the sanctuary and the Lady Chapel, and at St Davids the building of the magnificent nave was commenced under the Norman bishop Peter de Leia (1176–98) in the 1170s. Something of the Romanesque heritage of Wales may also be found in regions far from the centres of Norman power. His biographer states that Gruffudd ap Cynan caused Gwynedd to be strewn with churches as the firmament is strewn with stars. The church of Llanbadarn Fawr near Llandrindod has a strange early twelfth-century tympanum featuring two leaping lion-like creatures and a doorway rich in fantasy. Even more remarkable is the shrine at Pennant Melangell in the heart of the Berwyn Mountains; dating from about 1160 nothing comparable to it has survived anywhere else in Britain.

The shrine at Pennant Melangell in the Berwyn Mountains dates from about 1160, and is a quite remarkable Romanesque survival (Keith Hewitt: Country Life Picture Library).

Set in the Vale of Ewias, 'no more than three arrow-shots in width', the Augustinian priory of Llanthony is perhaps the most beautifully located of all the monasteries of Wales.

The church, cloister and monastic buildings at Llanthony were surrounded by a large precinct, now defined by earthworks.

The religious fervour which sprang from the efforts to reform the Church gave rise to new monastic orders. By 1170, the order of Cluny had two houses in Wales; so did the Black Canons, the observers of the *Rule of St Augustine*, while the order of Tiron had three. Among the Augustinian houses was Llanthony, perhaps the most beautifully located of all the monasteries of Wales. Far more numerous were the daughter houses of the monastery of Cîteaux in Burgundy. Wales was eventually to have thirteen Cistercian houses, seven of which were established before 1170. Unlike the Benedictines, who settled under the shadow of the power of the invaders, the Cistercians chose to build their monasteries 'far from the concourse of men'. Not only were they seekers of solitude, they were also creators of solitude, for they were not beyond depopulating the districts in their immediate vicinity. Of the Cistercian houses of Wales, the fabric of half of them has almost totally disappeared; the remains of the others, however, are among the most important indicators of the architectural achievements of the medieval makers of Wales. Among them is the nave of the abbey church at Margam, founded in 1147. This wonderful building bears eloquent testimony to the austerity of the early Cistercian ideal throughout Europe. The patrons of Cistercian abbeys endowed them with great tracts of land; Strata Florida, for example, came to own vast swathes of territory in the upper Teifi and Tywi valleys, land well suited to sheep-rearing, the characteristic activity of the Cistercians.

Alongside the growth of Latin monasticism was the recasting of the territorial organization of the Welsh Church. By 1170, the four dioceses of Wales had clear boundaries and their bishops were part of a defined hierarchy recognizing the archbishop of Canterbury as metropolitan. The boundaries drew on old traditions, and they therefore had a significance beyond the ecclesiastical; diocesan boundaries, for example, frequently coincided with changes in dialect and in legal and social practices. The process of defining the basic ecclesiastical units — the parishes — proved more protracted. It was afoot in the Vale of Glamorgan by 1100 but up to two centuries were to elapse before it had been completed throughout Wales. A parish represented a territory capable of maintaining a priest, and the network of parishes which eventually came into existence generally reflects the settlement pattern of twelfth- and thirteenth-century Wales. Originally created to serve the Church, parishes developed secular roles, serving as units of local government, taxation, relief of the poor and the compilation of population statistics, roles that continued to be of significance well into the twentieth century.

To a varying degree, sheep-rearing was significant to the economy of all thirteen Cistercian abbeys situated throughout medieval Wales. Vast upland sheep ranches existed in some areas, with sheep-cots spread throughout the landscape. This fourteenth-century manuscript illustration shows a man and woman tending sheep. In the Anglo-Norman centuries, the Cistercians would have employed their lay brothers to tend their flocks (The British Library, Additional Ms. 42130, f. 163v).

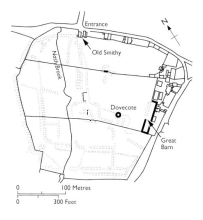

The key to Cistercian agricultural success was their system of grange farming. Wherever possible, their lands were consolidated in cohesive granges exploited from a single farm. Monknash, in the Vale of Glamorgan, is one of the best preserved grange centres in the country. This plan and the aerial photograph show the extent of the surviving buildings and earthworks. Anything up to 850 acres (350ha) of Cistercian land belonging to Neath Abbey surrounded this grange (Photograph, Crown Copyright: The Royal Commission on the Ancient and Historical Monuments of Wales).

THE HIGH MIDDLE AGES

THE MAKING OF WALES 1170–1348

Between 1170 and 1348 the developments apparent in the early twelfth century became increasingly marked. With the continuing rise in population, rural settlement intensified, resulting in a vast expansion in the exploitation of the waste. Urban settlement burgeoned, with new towns being created and existing ones adding to their inhabitants. Romanesque architecture evolved into Early and Decorated Gothic, the styles of most of the monasteries of Wales and many of the country's parish churches. The era saw the climax of castle-building, for, with the exception of Raglan, all the great castles of Wales belong to the period 1170–1348. The definition and intensification of lordship, over land as well as over men, continued apace. In *Pura Wallia* it led to the rise of the power of Gwynedd under Llywelyn ab Iorwerth (d. 1240) and Llywelyn ap Gruffudd (d. 1282), proof that there existed in medieval Wales the basic constituents of a Welsh polity. The effort to create such a polity reached its climax in 1267, when Llywelyn ap Gruffudd won recognition as prince of Wales; his ambitions received a severe blow in 1277 and were utterly destroyed in 1282–83. Llywelyn's principality became the royal counties of Wales, with which the heir to the English throne was invested. Yet the marcher lordships, whose *raison d'être* was to act as a cordon sanitaire between the kingdom of England and the territories of the Welsh rulers, continued in existence, and thus the division of Wales, first apparent in the late eleventh and early twelfth centuries, was perpetuated.

Of all these developments, the most significant in terms of the history of the Welsh landscape was the intensification of rural settlement, a feature of both Anglo-Norman and native Wales. In the March, place-names containing the element New- became increasingly common — Newton Nottage in Glamorgan, for example, and New Moat in Pembroke. The creation of new settlements involved a determined attack upon woodland, causing the

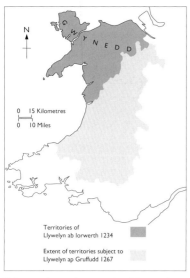

This map shows the strength of the royal house of Gwynedd under Llywelyn ab Iorwerth (d. 1240) and Llywelyn ap Gruffudd (d. 1282). The reassertion of Welsh authority under these two gifted rulers, and the response this provoked in the marcher lordships, led to a climax in castle-building across Wales as a whole.

thirteenth century to represent the climax of medieval assartment. In Anglesey, so great were the efforts of the assarters that the island was virtually denuded of trees. The right to assart was almost a condition of existence; when King Henry III (1216–72) seized much of north-east Wales in the 1240s, that was the right its inhabitants were chiefly concerned that the king should confirm.

Land could also be won for farming through drainage schemes. The monks of Tintern drained parts of the Caldicot Levels and the tenants of the lord of Gwynllŵg undertook similar work on the Wentlooge Levels. The ruling class was determined that some areas should not be brought under cultivation, for the chief delight of its members was the chase, and by establishing hunting parks they contributed to the preservation of ancient landscapes. The Norman lords of Abergavenny created a great park including much of the Sugar Loaf Mountain, and William de Braose (d. 1290), lord of Gower, surrounded 500 acres (200ha) at Parc le Breos with a 4 mile (6.4km) fence. Other areas were lost to cultivation through natural disasters. Coastal erosion created sunken forests at Newgale, and blown sand inundated Kenfig and part of Merthyr Mawr, as well as extensive areas of south-west Anglesey.

An aerial view of the village of St Brides Wentlooge, on the Wentlooge Levels to the north-east of Cardiff, taken in 1974. The village stands at the edge of drained and reclaimed peat deposits, with the process of drainage and land management already underway in the Roman period. The channels were maintained throughout the Middle Ages, with additional areas drained and reclaimed (Committee for Aerial Photography, Cambridge University).

Hunting parks, beloved by the ruling classes, were a prominent feature in the Welsh landscape of the High Middle Ages. This huge ditch is part of the enclosure defining the great park created by the lords of Abergavenny on the flanks of Sugar Loaf Mountain.

Excavations at Cefn Graeanog near Clynnog Fawr recovered evidence of a substantial twelfth- to thirteenth-century farmstead, comprising a house, barn, stable and byre (Gwynedd Archaeological Trust).

Central to the Welsh economy of the late thirteenth century was the rearing of cattle, the drawers of ploughs as well as a source of milk, meat and leather. This manuscript illustration comes from a thirteenth-century Welsh Lawbook (National Library of Wales, Peniarth Ms. 28, f. 23v).

The landscape surrounding the abbey ruins at Strata Florida is almost as rural today as when the monks were at the forefront of sheep-rearing and wool production.

Right: With the granting of extensive upland areas in Wales to the Cistercians, large parts of these lands became the domain of sheep. This map highlights the lands of Strata Florida Abbey, but also shows other Cistercian estates in south-west Wales.

Much of the new farming land was devoted to arable cultivation. In the 1290s, three quarters of the taxpayers of lowland Llŷn grew corn, mainly in the form of oats. The large barn built at Cefn Graeanog near Clynnog Fawr is evidence of the growing role of cereals, and the Welsh Lawbooks provide increasingly detailed instructions concerning joint ploughing, a necessity on land held in intermingling strips. Despite the rise in cereal-growing, Wales remained a country of mixed farming. Central to the economy was the rearing of cattle — the drawers of ploughs as well as a source of milk, meat and leather — and it is the cattle-rearers, above all, who have ensured that the Wales we have inherited is largely a land of grass. Although few of the early medieval pastures were enclosed, Wales was eventually to become very much a country of hedged pastures, and some of these hedges may be very old indeed. Hooper's theory — that the age of a hedge may be determined by the number of species of trees and shrubs it contains — is considered to be unreliable where western Britain is concerned. However, further hedge studies may permit many of the hedges of Wales to be dated with a degree of accuracy, and it is likely that some at least date back to the High Middle Ages, or even earlier.

The traditional role of the uplands was to provide summer grazing for cattle. With the granting of extensive estates to the Cistercians, large parts of them became the domain of the sheep. Sheep are admirably designed to prevent the growth of trees. Goats are even more effective, and they were a significant element in the livestock — the so-called wild goats of Snowdonia preserve the characteristics of medieval breeds. Rabbits, a twelfth-century introduction to Britain, are also eager grazers. Medieval rabbits differed from their modern descendants; they were incapable of digging burrows, and, as they were appreciated as a delicacy, warrens or pillow mounds were created

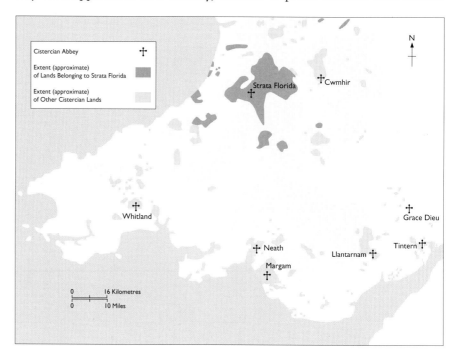

Wales has some 140 known examples of moated settlement sites, with the majority of them constructed between 1200 and 1325. In most cases, the moated island housed a manorial or sub-manorial residence, and the moat served as a symbol of the owner's status; though they were also a source of fish. Hen Gwrt in northern Monmouthshire is a well-preserved example.

This aerial view reveals the earthwork remains of the moated site in a field known as 'chapel garth', near Hanmer, to the south-east of Wrexham (Crown Copyright: The Royal Commission on the Ancient and Historical Monuments of Wales, 95-CS-0155).

for them. Other additions to the diet included pigeons, which were prized also for their manure; there is a splendid columbarium or dovecot at Cadoxton Court near Barry, and they are particularly numerous in the villages around Haverfordwest and Pembroke. Fish was an essential food. Wales has 140 moated sites; most of them were constructed between 1200 and 1325 and were primarily status symbols; they were also a source of fish, as were the Wye weirs owned by the monks of Tintern.

The rural expansion of the High Middle Ages coincided with a remarkable increase in the number of towns and of town-dwellers. Town planning in medieval Wales entered its last phase in the wake of the wars of King Edward I (1272–1307). Aberystwyth, Flint and Rhuddlan, established after the war of 1277, were the first of Edward's foundations. At Aberystwyth, an area of some 50 acres (20ha) had been enclosed by walls by 1280. Flint, protected by a bank and palisade rather than a wall, had a remarkably regular layout inspired by the *bastides* of Gascony. Its six parallel streets and one cross route can still be traced today. Rhuddlan, like Flint, was not a walled town, but the earthworks which defended its northern corner are still visible.

The apogee of medieval town planning in Wales followed in the wake of the wars of King Edward I. Nine new royal boroughs came into existence, with plans inspired by the bastides of Gascony. Pride of place must be accorded to Conwy, with the town walls and castle raised in a frenzied building-programme of the 1280s. The layout and street plan were determined at the very outset, and seen from the air it is clear that the town walls continue to determine the shape of the borough today.

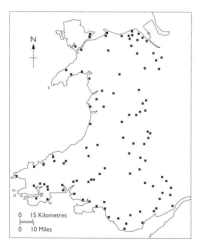

The towns of medieval Wales.

After the war of 1282–83 Edward was far more ambitious, for in the 1280s his builders constructed walled towns which rank among the most remarkable in Europe. Pride of place must be accorded to Conwy, where the town walls are among the most splendid of the achievements of the makers of Wales. Some 1,400 yards (1,280m) in length, defended by twenty-one towers and pierced by three double-towered gateways, they are a far more ambitious project than the 800-feet (730m) wall surrounding the town of Caernarfon. Among the most intriguing features of Conwy's defences is the row of twelve privies west of the Mill Gate, an unique multiple sanitary arrangement built to serve the needs of the king's Wardrobe, the royal secretariat which was located at Conwy in the mid 1280s.

In the late thirteenth and early fourteenth centuries, nine royal boroughs came into existence in Wales, either as new foundations or as existing settlements brought into the burgal fold. In addition, a similar number was established by seigneurial fiat. By 1309, when the last of the creations — the borough of Bala — was founded, Wales had 109 settlements with at least some pretensions to burgal status. Up to half of them either failed or only achieved stunted growth. At New Radnor, a 25-acre (10ha) settlement laid out in the late thirteenth century, not all its original plots are occupied even today. Cefnllys, established by the Mortimer family in Maelienydd, has long been totally abandoned.

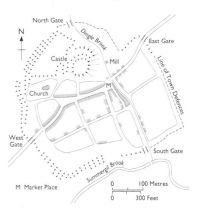

New Radnor was a planted town probably first laid out in the late thirteenth century. Its initial growth was rapid, with up to 189 burgesses or townsmen recorded in 1304. The plan of the borough shows the extent of early ambitions, but today the modern town is less densely developed than its medieval counterpart. The urban fringe remains essentially rural.

Of the successful towns, the great majority were situated in the southern coastlands; the Edwardian boroughs were small, for the magnificence of their fortifications bore little relationship to their size. Cardiff, with its 421 burgages, was the largest of the Welsh towns of the High Middle Ages; by 1300 it had spilled out beyond the confines of its defences and spawned the extramural settlement of Crockherbtown. Similar growth occurred in other towns, Abergavenny, Carmarthen, Haverfordwest and Pembroke among them. Street alignments emerged which would still dominate the townscapes of the twentieth century. The wide central street of Carmarthen marks the site of the medieval cattle-market, and comparable features may be seen at Monmouth, Brecon and elsewhere. Monmouth can also boast of one of the most attractive of Wales's medieval buildings — the fortified bridge erected across the river Monnow in the late thirteenth century. Other surviving defences added in that period to Welsh towns of Norman provenance include the walls and gatehouse at Chepstow, the barbican at Tenby and the south gatehouse at Kidwelly.

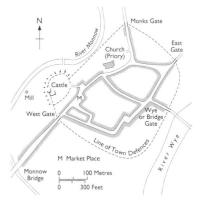

Monmouth was one of the earliest Norman towns established in Wales. Its growth was steady and was sustained by the success of its market function. From the late thirteenth to early fourteenth centuries the initial defences were replaced by stone walls, with four gates. An extra-mural suburb extended down to the river Monnow, where a superb fortified bridge was built in 1272.

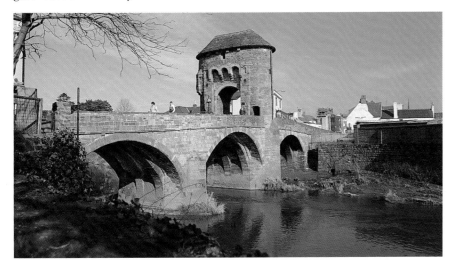

While the town walls of Chepstow, and even more so those of Conwy and Caernarfon, are impressive, they are overshadowed by the splendours of the castles that are associated with them. Wales's thirteenth-century castles are its greatest architectural monuments, and the fact that the country's most distinguished buildings are the product of its subjection is a paradox commented upon by the eighteenth-century topographical writer, Thomas Pennant, who described Wales's Edwardian castles as 'the magnificent badges of our subjection'. Admittedly, some of the most appealing fortifications —Castell y Bere, Dinas Brân and Dolwyddelan among them — were built by the Welsh princes, but all the most elaborate castles were erected under the auspices of the English king or of those of his barons who held marcher lordships.

Among the baronial castles are Pembroke, with its imposing round tower, Chepstow and Kidwelly, with their superb spur buttresses, the magnificently sited castles of Llansteffan, Cilgerran and Carreg Cennen (the last originally a Welsh castle but rebuilt by the Giffard family), and Grosmont, Skenfrith, and White, the 'three castles' of northern Gwent in their delightfully verdant settings. Even more outstanding is Caerphilly, a castle site among the largest in Europe. With its water defences, its fortified dam and its island castle, it is the earliest and most elaborate example of a concentric fortification. Almost as remarkable is Denbigh, where the great gatehouse with its three octagonal towers is a masterpiece of military architecture.

Wales's thirteenth-century castles are perhaps its greatest architectural monuments. Some of the most appealing were those fortifications raised by the native Welsh princes, including Castell y Bere in the magnificent landscape northeast of Tywyn.

One of the most charming baronial castles of the thirteenth century can be seen at Skenfrith in northern Monmouthshire. Initially raised by Hubert de Burgh (d. 1243), a small town also existed around St Bridget's church.

It is possible that the Denbigh gatehouse was designed by James of St George, Master of the King's Works, and architect of Edward I's Welsh castles. A Savoyard, Master James incorporated in his castles features drawn from his Alpine home, as well as from Byzantium, the Crusader lands and the French domains of the English and French kings. Edward ordered the construction *de novo* of seven castles in Wales and the rebuilding or enlargement of several others. Of the seven, Flint has a fortified keep or freestanding *donjon*, a concept which was outmoded by the late thirteenth century. Four of the castles — Aberystwyth, Rhuddlan, Harlech and Beaumaris — are concentric fortifications in the tradition of Caerphilly; indeed Beaumaris, built on a level and therefore unconstricted site, is the epitome of symmetric perfection. At Conwy and Caernarfon, where castle and town walls are superbly integrated, concentricity was abandoned in favour of massive curtain walls and monumental gateways. Conwy, considered by Sir Goronwy Edwards to be 'incomparably the most magnificent of Edward I's Welsh castles', consists of two adjoining wards each flanked by a barbican. The layout at Caernarfon is not dissimilar; Caernarfon's distinction lies in its magnitude. At some 580 feet (180m) across, it is nearly 200 feet (60m) longer than Conwy. Caernarfon stands out, too, in its echoes of Byzantium — deliberate expressions of its imperial role. Conceived of as a coherent strategy to secure conquest and built under common supervision, the unity of Master James's work makes him one of the most remarkable of the makers of Wales.

Harlech was one of a group of completely new castles built for King Edward I at the end of the thirteenth century. Today, it is one of the most familiar strongholds in the British Isles.

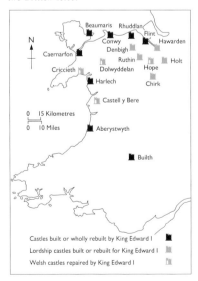

Castle-building during the Edwardian campaigns in Wales in the late thirteenth century.

Successive bishops of St Davids were to prove avid builders in the High Middle Ages. The handsome chambers at Lamphey near Pembroke date from the later thirteenth to mid-fourteenth centuries. The palace here was at the centre of a major estate.

Edward I's Welsh castles represented an expenditure of almost £100,000, well over twice the king's regular annual income. In addition, his father and grandfather spent thousands of pounds on castles in Wales, as did the leading lords of the March. The High Middle Ages saw an equivalent if not a greater expenditure on monastic buildings, those of the Cistercians in particular. Most of the Welsh Cistercian abbey churches were built between 1170 and 1230. They offer evidence of the simplicity favoured by the early Cistercians and of the evolution of ecclesiastical architecture from Romanesque through to Early Gothic. Some abbey churches were rebuilt on a far more magnificent scale. Among them were Tintern (about 1269–1301) and Neath (about 1280–1330), where the influence of the Decorated French Gothic style early employed at Westminster Abbey is apparent. Of the churches of other monastic orders, the most impressive is that of the Benedictines at Brecon, where the chancel is a superb example of Early Gothic. In addition, Brecon has Wales's only substantial remains of a medieval friary — the Dominican house now incorporated within the buildings of Christ College.

The High Middle Ages also saw extensive building by the secular wing of the Church. All four of the ancient cathedrals of Wales contain important work of the period. In addition, the bishops of St Davids were avid builders of great houses — the hall at Llawhaden, the palace at Lamphey and the bishop's palace at St Davids, described by Glanmor Williams as 'the most beautiful building [erected] in Wales in the Middle Ages'. Above all, the years 1170 to 1348 were a period of intense construction of parish churches. Of the hundreds of churches built in Wales in those years, some of the remoter ones, such as Rhulen in Radnorshire, are so unassuming that it is difficult to assign them to any particular style. In the wealthier parts of Wales, churches with sturdy towers proliferated; those at Cheriton in Gower and at Cowbridge in the Vale of Glamorgan are among the most attractive examples. Town churches were particularly subject to the church-rebuilding boom of the late Middle Ages, but work from the period 1170–1348 may be found at Brecon, Tenby, Newport and elsewhere.

The growth of towns and the rebuilding of churches are an indication of the growing prosperity of Wales by the late thirteenth century. There was an expansion in trade, landward and seaward, and the mineral resources of Wales — lead in Flintshire and iron and coal in the south — were being increasingly exploited. The wool produced by the flocks of the uplands, which had originally been exported as fleeces, began to be processed in Wales, and by 1350 the country had at least seventy-five fulling mills. These developments tended to undermine the rigid social divisions of earlier centuries, a change assisted by the decline in the number of manors worked by bond labour, at least in the regions which until 1282 constituted *Pura Wallia*. The tax records of 1292–93 show that in Merioneth freemen outnumbered bondmen by four to one, and by then absolute villeinage had almost disappeared from most of central and south-west Wales. By the early fourteenth century, demesne farming was being abandoned in *Marchia Wallie* also; this further blurred the distinction between the free and the unfree, a development which had an impact upon settlement patterns.

Even greater was the impact of the growth of population. By 1300, Wales had at least 300,000 inhabitants. The free population of *Pura Wallia* could be remarkably prolific. The land of Iorwerth ap Cadwgan, who flourished in the 1220s, was by 1313 shared among twenty-seven of his descendants. Chronic overcrowding of the original descendants' lands could be avoided by carving out new holdings. By 1334, the descendants of Edryd ap Marchudd, who originated in Abergele, had fifteen settlements extending from Betws y Coed to Bodelwyddan. The inhabitants of *Marchia Wallie* could also be prolific. By the early fourteenth century, the tenant families of upland Hay held less than 2 acres (0.8ha) of arable land apiece, and similar patterns of rural overpopulation could be found in the lordships of Monmouth and Brecon. Population growth was aided by the colonists attracted to Wales in the wake of the Edwardian conquest. At least 20,000 acres (8,000ha) of the Vale of Clwyd were cleared of their Welsh proprietors, and around the royal boroughs further clearances provided land for the immigrant burgesses. The incomers came from areas of intense arable agriculture and they boosted the proportion of land in Wales subject to the plough.

The prosperity apparent in Wales by 1300 was precarious. Population growth had driven families to settle on indifferent land and thus communities were being pushed to the margins of cultivable soil. Imbalance between arable and livestock husbandry could lead to serious problems of soil exhaustion. Animal diseases such as the sheep scab epidemic of 1291 could drive entire communities over the abyss. There is evidence by the early fourteenth century that the period of favourable climate which began around 1080 was coming to an end. Appalling weather between 1315 and 1318 caused a great famine across Europe. The Hundred Years' War began in 1337 and led to heavy taxation and the collapse of the currency. And there was worse to come.

The growth of towns, and a thriving market economy led to an increase in the exploitation of mineral resources in Wales, with iron important in the south. This manuscript illustration shows smiths of the High Middle Ages at work at the forge (The British Library, Sloane Ms. 3983, f. 5).

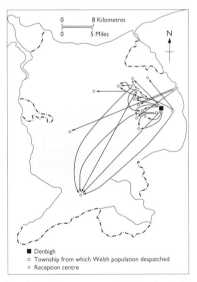

The Edwardian conquest of Wales attracted new English colonists. Around Denbigh, for example, large areas of the Vale of Clwyd were cleared of their Welsh proprietors to provide land for the immigrant settlers. Consequently, as this simplified map shows, there were highly significant movements of population (After Owen 1989).

THE LATER MIDDLE AGES

THE MAKING OF WALES 1348–1536

In Wales, as in the rest of Europe, the Later Middle Ages were ushered in by the Black Death. Carried by the fleas of the black rat, bubonic and pneumonic plague killed about a third of the inhabitants of the Old World between 1347 and 1350. Twenty-five million people died in Europe alone, and the pestilence struck again and again, particularly in 1361 and 1369. The cataclysm may not have been as severe in Wales as elsewhere, for the death toll was highest in large towns and in thickly populated lowland districts. Nevertheless, the plague had a profound effect upon the country's settlement pattern and social organization. The number of inhabitants — probably in decline since the 1310s — slumped; indeed, it was to take at least two hundred and fifty years before the population of Wales would again be as large as it had been at the opening of that decade.

The implications of demographic decline were far-reaching. Borough plantation became a thing of the past and existing towns contracted. As population pressure eased, there was a retreat from the more marginal lands, the inhabitants of which had dwelt in scattered settlements rather than in villages. Wales does not have deserted villages in numbers or size comparable with the Midlands of England, where villages were abandoned in their hundreds. Nevertheless, deserted villages have been identified in parts of the Welsh lowlands — in the neighbourhood of Barry, for example, and at Eglwys Gymyn near Laugharne and Runston near Chepstow. The exodus from them was not as sudden as was once believed; Runston still had a few inhabitants as late as the eighteenth century.

As villages of unfree tenants became depopulated by disease and migration, the scattered strips of villein holdings began to be reorganized into consolidated farms. Similar developments occurred in the lands of the free population as death from pestilence slowed down the division of property among numerous male heirs and as the land of a man dying without heirs escheated to his lord. Ambitious members of Welsh gentry families were anxious to be released from what they considered to be the restrictions of traditional Welsh

tenure; they wished to hold land according to English Law, thus permitting them to accumulate property and to bequeath it to a single heir. The contraction in the labour force gave the final quietus to the direct farming of demesne land and as a result the lords of the March came to have a tenuous connection with their Welsh territories. This created a vacuum which the emerging Welsh gentry were eager to fill. The Black Death greatly aided the process whereby social division based on legal rank was yielding to social division based upon wealth. Implicit in the change was the replacement of the holdings of the free and the unfree by a pattern of landed estates, and the creation of a society consisting of a few wealthy proprietors, a multitude of property-less tenants and an underclass of pauperized cottagers. This was the society which eventually came into being over the greater part of Wales, a development which had a profound impact upon the appearance of the country.

Throughout Europe, the authorities, lay and clerical, reacted to the crisis of the late fourteenth century by subjecting the mass of the population to ruthlessly exploitative lordship. Resentment of exploitation and of the curtailing of ancient liberties was a European-wide phenomenon. In Wales it had an extra dimension, arising from the animosity of a conquered people towards its foreign lords, an animosity which found expression in the severe unrest of the 1340s, the hopes in the 1370s of deliverance through Owain Lawgoch (d. 1378), great-nephew of Llywelyn ap Gruffudd, and, above all, in that astonishing insurgence, the revolt of Owain Glyndŵr (1400–10).

The devastation wrought during the Glyndŵr revolt swept away any amelioration that the Welsh economy might have undergone since the Black Death. Both sides were involved in depredation, for while Glyndŵr was accused of 'bringing all things to waste', the English king was said to have 'proclaimed "havoc" of the whole of Wales'. At least forty towns suffered severely; Cardiff took centuries to recover, and such were the ravages visited upon Nefyn that it never regained its earlier prosperity. The cathedrals of Bangor and St Asaph were partially destroyed, as were scores of parish churches. Royal troops razed the friary at Llanfaes, burial-place of Joan, wife of Llywelyn ab Iorwerth, and at Strata Florida the abbey buildings became a barracks and the church a stable. So despoiled was the Cistercian monastery at Margam that the monks were obliged to roam like vagabonds. Mills were destroyed, houses and crops burnt and the huge communal fines imposed upon the rebellious Welsh pauperized entire communities. The racial discrimination against the Welsh which had partially fuelled the revolt was institutionalized as a result of it, for the Penal Laws of 1401–02 — although frequently ignored in subsequent decades — gave the inferior status of the Welsh the endorsement of statute. Developments discernible in Welsh society at least since the Black Death, such as the depopulation of the hamlets and villages of the unfree tenants and the concentration of land in fewer hands, were accelerated by the revolt; so much so that, by the mid-fifteenth century, a pattern of settlement, of trade and of economic organization was emerging which was to dominate Wales until the country was transformed by the growth of industry over three hundred years later.

The Anglo-Norman village of Barry was a linear settlement adjacent to the castle of the de Barri family. After the second half of the fourteenth century, the village was reduced to about half its former size. Three of its twelfth- to fourteenth-century houses were excavated in 1962–77, with one of these seen in the photograph. The plan shows all three plots at the centre (Photograph: Glamorgan-Gwent Archaeological Trust).

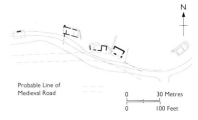

Probable Line of Medieval Road

0   30 Metres
0   100 Feet

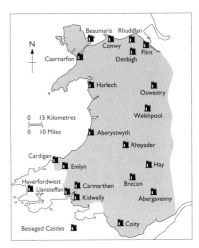

The regions subject to Owain Glyndŵr at the height of the Welsh revolt in 1404–05. Major castles subject to Welsh siege are also shown.

Weobley Castle on the Gower peninsula was essentially a fortified manor house first built in the early fourteenth century. It was remodelled in the 1490s by the great Sir Rhys ap Thomas (d. 1525).

The Glyndŵr revolt led to a renewed interest in fortification. In 1414, the burgesses of Beaumaris were given permission to surround their town with walls; in the following year walls were built to protect the eastern suburbs of Carmarthen and at much the same time Ruthin and Kidwelly were girded with defensive ditches. Most of the castles of the Principality were in the hands of the Crown, and as the fifteenth century advanced that became true of many of the castles of the March also. They underwent a degree of strengthening and repair; the gatehouse at Carmarthen Castle, for example, was rebuilt around 1410. More extensive building occurred at those castles occupied permanently or intermittently by their owners. The Beauchamp lords of Glamorgan constructed a range of buildings along the western curtain wall at Cardiff in the 1430s, and twenty years later the Stradlings built a south range at St Donat's Castle. In the same period, the lords of Chirk added a south range to their castle and in the 1490s Rhys ap Thomas (d. 1525) remodelled much of the castles of Carew and Weobley. In addition, there were more modest fortified buildings — tower houses such as those at Angle, Broncoed, Talgarth and Scethrog, although some of these may date originally from the fourteenth century.

Far and away the most elaborate fortified complex built in Wales — indeed, built in Britain — in the fifteenth century was the castle at Raglan. The Great Tower, a self-contained fortress in its own right, and the south gate were built between 1435 and 1445 by Sir William ap Thomas (d. 1445). The buildings around the two great courts, erected in the 1460s, were the work of his son, William Herbert (d. 1469), one of the first Welshmen to adopt a permanent surname; although the courtyard buildings, especially those on the

Raglan Castle in Monmouthshire is far and away the most elaborate fortified complex built in Wales in the fifteenth century. The Great Tower, in the centre distance of this view, was a self-contained fortress in its own right. Two large courtyards housed the chambers and lodgings commensurate with the status of a family of rank.

north side, were extensively remodelled by Herbert's great-grandson, William Somerset (d. 1589), in the late sixteenth century, Raglan still retains the essential shape it had when William Herbert was executed in 1469. With its delightful pastoral setting, its great bulk, its superb machicolations and its ingenious gateway defences, Raglan is perhaps the most fascinating of all the medieval buildings of Wales. Among its features are gunloops and gun embrasures, for the castle was built after the invention of gunpowder and is thus something of an anachronism.

The house of Raglan rose to prominence and riches through its support of the Yorkists in the dynastic struggle which shook the territories of the Crown of England in the later fifteenth century. Yet, although the 'Wars of the Roses' lasted over thirty years (1455–87), the two factions were engaged in arms for a total of only thirteen weeks; thus, the dislocation caused by the 'Wars' can be exaggerated. Exaggerated, too, is the notion of fifteenth-century Wales as a country uniquely racked by racial bitterness and anarchy. Although Welsh poetry provides ample evidence of Anglophobia and English sources offer many examples of suspicion and hatred of the Welsh, the need peacefully to coexist was paramount, and, as the decades passed, barriers between the Welsh and the English were being eroded, at least among the members of the upper layers of society. Although government in Wales was much fragmented and complaints of maladministration legion, the tendency to portray the country as a haven of criminals has been carried to excess. Older historians were wont to suggest that violence and lawlessness came under control following the advent of the Tudor dynasty in 1485, but there is evidence that decades before this date the economy was reviving and people were living in an increasingly secure environment.

Architecture provides the most telling evidence. Although the Raglan family built a castle, the motive was as much flamboyance as defence. There was building work at some of the older castles, but the main aim was to add to domestic comfort rather than to the fortifications. Some early Tudor houses — in particular Llancaiach Fawr near Gelligaer – have fascinating defensive features, but Welsh housebuilders were increasingly content with non-fortified dwellings. While there are 400 tower-houses in County Limerick and hundreds in Cumberland and Northumberland, there are less than a score in the whole of Wales.

The confidence which allowed the fortress mentality to be abandoned when building had profound implications for the making of Wales, for it meant the emergence of a landscape dotted with mansions rather than castles, and with towns free from restrictive defences. It also meant, as Peter Smith has put it, that 'the distinction between a military caste, safe behind battlements, and a peasant class, living in undefended cottages, started to fade, and the mainstream of domestic architecture began to flow in quite another direction, in the direction of buildings undistorted by the necessities of war'.

A study of surviving early houses suggests that their numbers are in inverse proportion to the number of castles. Thus, the historic county of Glamorgan has far fewer early houses than that of Denbighshire. There, as elsewhere in northern and eastern Wales, the dominant late-medieval type was the hall-

Very few small, fortified dwellings were built in Wales after the thirteenth century. The tower house — common in Scotland and Ireland — was comparatively rare. This is one of the few surviving examples, situated at Angle in Pembrokeshire (Crown Copyright: The Royal Commission on the Ancient and Historical Monuments of Wales).

Opposite: *In northern and eastern Wales, the dominant type of late medieval dwelling was the hall-house. Cochwillan near Bethesda, with its hammer-beam wooden roof, is seen as a grand finale of the upper-class hall. The house was probably built by Gwilym ap Gruffudd (d. 1500) who was made high sheriff of Caernarvonshire by King Henry VII.*

Below: *Ground plan of Cochwillan showing how the hall dominated the entire house (After Smith 1988).*

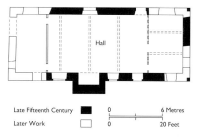

Late Fifteenth Century	0	6 Metres
Later Work	0	20 Feet

house, 'a great lofty room, its timbers disappearing into the darkness of a roof blackened by the smoke from an open hearth and ventilated by draughts from glassless windows'. Among the most interesting of Wales's fifteenth-century hall-houses are Bryndraenog in Radnorshire, with its magnificent cruck trusses, Great House, also in Radnorshire, the widest cruck hall in Wales at 28 feet (8.6m), Hafod, near Llansilin — an aisle-truss hall — and Cochwillan near Bethesda, with its splendid hammer-beam roof. But of all the medieval houses of Wales undoubtedly the most appealing is Tretower, the hall-house built by Sir Roger Vaughan (d. 1471) between 1457 and 1470 in the enchanting valley of the Rhiangoll.

These houses were all gentry dwellings of generous proportions. More significant as an indicator of prosperity are the fifteenth-century houses of less exalted members of society. That century was the first in which significant numbers of the common people had the means to acquire durable houses. Such houses were beyond the means of the mass of the population; they continued to live in impermanent dwellings of mud and wattle, forerunners of buildings which housed a significant proportion of the inhabitants of impoverished Cardiganshire until very recent times. The durable habitations of at least some people below the gentry level point to the emergence, by about 1450, of a yeoman class. This was the consequence, no doubt, of the ability of its members to profit from the greater availability of land which resulted from the tribulations of the previous century. The great majority of the yeoman dwellings are to be found in north-east Wales, where their existence helps to explain why that region was so prominent in the literary and religious life of Wales in the century and more after 1450. Most of them are timber-framed buildings; indeed, three-quarters of the Welsh houses surviving from before the 1530s are of half-timbered 'black and white' construction. Their walls were prefabricated by skilled carpenters, virtually an assembly-line system which brought a reasonable dwelling within reach of a large number of people.

Tretower Court, near Crickhowell, is undoubtedly the most appealing medieval house surviving in Wales. It was built by the Yorkist supporter, Sir Roger Vaughan, in the years before his death in 1471. The photograph shows Sir Roger's great hall, situated in the western range, and the courtyard plan shows the full extent of the house.

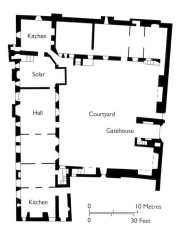

0	10 Metres
0	30 Feet

In the later Middle Ages, and for centuries after, the carpenter much outshone the mason in the north and east of Wales. Half-timbered buildings continue to sparkle across the landscape of this region. Cefnllyfnog in Powys began as a late medieval hall-house, and was remodelled with the storeyed cross-wing in the foreground in the seventeenth century (Crown Copyright: The Royal Commission on the Ancient and Historical Monuments of Wales).

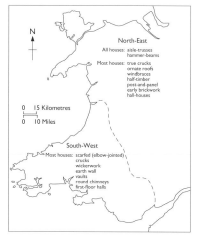

This simplified map shows the two broad building regions of Wales: to the north and east, timber was the most significant early material; to the south and west stone and earth walls were more common (After Smith 1988).

Half-timbered buildings were as common in the towns of north and east Wales as they were in the countryside. Most medieval urban buildings have sadly disappeared, with Ruthin as our last real reminder of a departed urban gaiety.

Although Wales seems rich in stone, little of it is of high building quality, for the country lacks anything comparable with the great oolitic belt which crosses England. Thus in the later Middle Ages, and for centuries to come, the carpenter much outshone the mason, and the whole of Wales north-east of a line from Machynlleth to Newport was the domain of the half-timbered building — a far more extensive region than surviving buildings would suggest. This was as true of the towns as of the countryside. From Beaumaris to Monmouth, the recovering towns of late fifteenth-century Wales sparkled with black and white houses, and would continue to do so until the early nineteenth century. Now, as Peter Smith sadly observes, only Ruthin remains. 'It should', he declares, 'be scrupulously preserved as a national monument, as our last reminder of a departed urban gaiety before it was effaced by the dull reign of stone and stucco'.

The hall-houses, the yeoman dwellings and the refurbishment of the towns all provide evidence of the revival of the Welsh economy in the late fifteenth century. Literary sources, in particular the very distinguished body of Welsh poetry produced in the century after 1450, are further evidence, for a society close to destitution is not one which can maintain the servants of the muse through the long years of their apprenticeship and provide them with the hospitality they crave. The Church also shared in the recovery, as the remarkable boom in church building in the late fifteenth and early sixteenth centuries testifies. Again the north-east led the way. Indeed, so extensive was the building and rebuilding in the Perpendicular style that much of the evidence of the region's earlier medieval churches has been almost wholly overshadowed. Ecclesiastical and domestic architecture developed in tandem. Fine timber roofs were the glory of hall-houses as they were of churches, and what was a hall-house with its step to the dais but a secular version of the church with its step to the altar? Wales's Celtic tradition of 'through' churches with no structural division between nave and chancel caused the similarity to be more marked there than elsewhere.

Among the delights of the north-east are the double-nave churches so characteristic of the Vale of Clwyd. Abergele is the largest of them, but Llanefydd, with its light and spacious feel, is perhaps the most attractive. The additional nave was probably built to accommodate an increasing population, but it may represent the desire to provide space in which to honour the burgeoning cult of the Virgin Mary. The most attractive religious building in the north-east is undoubtedly St Winifred's Well at Holywell, with its fine vaulting, its four-centred arches and its superb traceried screenwork — of which, alas, only fragments now remain. Completed in the first decade of the sixteenth century, it was built under the patronage of Margaret Beaufort (d. 1509), mother of King Henry VII (1485–1509) and wife of Lord Stanley. Other building work associated with her and her relations by marriage include the so-called 'Stanley churches' at Gresford, Mold, Northop, Holt and Wrexham, Wales's finest group of Perpendicular churches. Among their splendours are their towers, that of Wrexham in particular. Gresford, with its wonderful harmony of design, its glorious roof and its magnificent east window, is the finest parish church in Wales. Partly financed by the Stanleys, it could also draw upon the considerable income produced by its wonder-working image of the Virgin Mary.

The harmony in the design of the late fifteenth-century church at Gresford near Wrexham is striking. It is perhaps the finest parish church in Wales.

St Winifred's Well at Holywell in Flintshire is a quite remarkable structure, with stonework of the very highest quality. It was completed in the first years of the sixteenth century under the patronage of Margaret Beaufort, the mother of King Henry VII.

St Giles at Wrexham is one of the finest examples of town church rebuilding in the late fifteenth and early sixteenth centuries. The tower, probably by the master mason William Hort, is its greatest glory.

The building and rebuilding of town churches, of which Wrexham and Mold are such fine examples, was much in vogue in the years 1450 to 1530. Other major projects include St John's, Cardiff and St Cybi's, Holyhead, as well as extensive rebuilding work such as the chancel at Presteigne, the nave at Welshpool, the tower at St Mary's, Brecon, the roof, porch and north aisle at Tenby, St Anne's Chapel at Swansea and the clerestory at St Mary's, Haverfordwest. There was work also at the four cathedrals. Bangor and St Asaph were restored and remodelled; Llandaff was enhanced by the handsome Jasper Tower, built under the patronage of Jasper Tudor (d. 1495), uncle of Henry VII; St Davids acquired the superb Perpendicular chapel of Bishop Vaughan (1509–22) and received its crowning glory, the Irish oak ceiling of the nave, 'a work of almost Arabian gorgeousness'.

In this building activity, little resembling a Welsh style or styles is apparent. The Jasper Tower, St John's in Cardiff and a number of the handsome churches of southern Monmouthshire were in the tradition of the Somerset churches of which St Mary Magdalene, Taunton is the exemplar; Gresford was modelled upon the Perpendicular churches of the Cheshire Plain, although in quality it surpasses all of them; the Wrexham tower was inspired by that pinnacled marvel, the tower of St Peter's, Gloucester; Holyhead and other Gwynedd churches such as Llaneilian and Clynnog Fawr were the work of incoming craftsmen, probably those imported to undertake the work at Bangor Cathedral.

Nevertheless, some of the less ambitious churches of Wales — the dignified, unadorned towers of Defynnog and Talgarth, for example — do point to the existence of native craftsmen working in their own idiom. This is more pronounced among carpenters than among masons. Wales has only one church wholly built of timber — All Saints, Trelystan, splendidly situated on the slopes of the Long Mountain east of Welshpool. The country has, however, a wealth of timber bell-turrets, porches, roofs, screens and lofts. The screens and lofts are among the finest of all the creations of the makers of Wales. They are, stresses Glanmor Williams, the product of 'a strongly defined native tradition of woodworking', and he suggests that the carvers, confined, as they were, to 'a limited number of highly stylized themes and patterns', had close affinities with the Welsh poets, for 'in wood and in word, the flowing exuberance and vitality of the artist were enhanced rather than fettered by his strict adherence to the meticulous detail and the exacting classicism of his artistic endeavours'. Traces of over three hundred screens have been discovered in Wales. Only a few survive, and their destruction — particularly that of the most magnificent of them, the screen at Newtown — is one of the greatest blows suffered by the Welsh cultural heritage. Of those that do survive, probably the most appealing are the screens at Llanegryn, north of Tywyn, Llananno, north of Llandrindod, Llanfilo, near Brecon, and Patrisio, north of Abergavenny. Anyone seeing the screen at Patrisio, with its 'mysterious and charming silver patina', cannot but agree with Glanmor Williams that the traceries of a Welsh screen are 'as congenial an expression of Welsh medieval aesthetics as a *cywydd* or an *englyn*'.

Skill with timber underlines the central importance of woodlands in the

The skill of a native Welsh tradition of woodworking can be seen in numerous examples of late medieval church screens. Patrisio, north of Abergavenny, is one of the most celebrated examples, with the superb quality of the craftsmanship revealed in this detail.

The nave in the tiny parish church at Patrisio, where the carved wooden screen far outshines the simple architectural detail of the remainder.

By the 1530s, Cardiff was probably one of only five towns in Wales with a population of around 1,500. The layout and size of the town were probably very similar to the arrangements mapped by John Speed in 1610 (National Library of Wales).

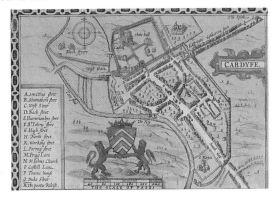

economy of late medieval Wales. They were the source not only of building material but also of fuel for heating and cooking, timber for furniture, charcoal for smelting, tannin for the leather industry, ashes for the dyeing and soap industries, soles for clogs, staves for barrels and the means of making a host of household utensils; in addition they offered game, the pleasures of the chase, pannage for pigs and shelter for outlaws. Yet, by the early sixteenth century, only about 15 per cent of the surface of Wales was forested, a percentage no higher than that of the High Middle Ages. Thus it would seem that any reafforestation that had occurred as a result of the fourteenth-century contraction in population had been reversed by the renewal of assartment in the following century. Woodlands still abounded along the borderlands, but in Anglesey, Pembrokeshire, Cardiganshire and the Vale of Glamorgan, anything resembling a forest had long disappeared. This did not mean that the landscape in those regions was treeless, for everywhere there were copses and wooded slopes, shade trees and hedgerow trees, almost all of them — in marked contrast to today — belonging to indigenous species.

Thus, by dint of the labour of countless generations of the makers of Wales, the country was by the 1530s largely a cleared landscape. It was described in that decade by the topographer John Leland, and detailed information is also available in the great survey of Church property — *Valor Ecclesiasticus* — compiled in 1535. The picture that emerges is that of a pre-industrial society based upon peasant farming, but with some significant secondary economic activity also based in the main upon agriculture. Compared with today, Wales in the 1530s was a sparsely populated country. It had perhaps 270,000 people, fewer than it had had in 1300 and less than a tenth of the present population. About 15 per cent were town-dwellers, compared with over 80 per cent today. Probably only five towns, Carmarthen, Brecon, Wrexham, Haverfordwest and Cardiff, had as many as 1,500 inhabitants, and in any case, town-dwellers, with their cattle

on the town lands and their backstreet sties and byres, were themselves half agriculturists.

In many ways, the countryside did not look markedly different from the way it looks today. It had fewer enclosed fields and hedgerows. George Owen claimed in 1603 that gavelkind 'had made the whole countrie to remain... without hedges and enclosures', and Rice Merrick stated in 1578 that, two generations previously, cattle could run to the sea without hindrance from the main road crossing the Vale of Glamorgan. Yet Leland noted that fields had been enclosed in Anglesey, and it is now accepted that there was extensive construction of boundary hedges in medieval Wales. The country was less uniformly green than it was to be in the late twentieth century, for corn was grown virtually everywhere. While corn produced 75 per cent of the tithe paid by the lowland parish of Newton Nottage, it was 20 per cent of that of the highland parish of Merthyr Tydfil, and the hills were dotted with barns and corn-mills. Virtually all the corn was grown for home consumption, for it was Wales's pastoral, not its arable, farming which produced the country's surpluses.

Sheep and cattle were virtually the sole source of income in the countryside. In many ways, sheep were the most important form of livestock. It was their grazing which prevented the reafforestation of the uplands and, as the mountains became increasingly the domain of sheep, transhumance declined, for sheep, when not milked — and they rarely were in Wales — do not need daily tendance. Although summer migration did not come to an end until about 1790, many *hafotai* had become independent farms by the early sixteenth century. Even more significant was the wealth produced by turning fleeces into cloth, for the cloth industry was a highly effective means of spreading wealth. The industry failed to prosper in the south-west, which probably explains the dearth of late medieval houses in that region. It flourished mightily in the north-east and was successful in the middle borderlands and the south-east, surely the key to the richness of those regions in early yeoman dwellings.

Sheep produce fleeces, meat and leather. Cattle produce meat, leather, horn, milk, butter and cheese. Leather-making, an important and underemphasized activity in pre-industrial Wales, made itself felt, olfactorily and otherwise, in all Welsh towns. Dairy products had a central role in the economy of lowland Wales, with Bristol drawing heavily on the output of the coastal south. The trade in beef cattle had a role almost everywhere. The droving of cattle to England for fattening and sale became well-established in the late fifteenth century, and as a result a pattern of roads was emerging which would strongly influence Welsh topography and serve to emphasize west–east, at the expense of north–south, communications. Cattle-droving would continue to be a central feature of the Welsh economy until the creation of Wales's railway network, little more than a century ago. It opened up vast areas of remote country, led to the establishment of scores of forges and taverns and was the chief ultimate source of the wealth which permitted Welsh landlords to build their mansions, lay out their parks and, in a myriad other ways, leave their impress upon the land of Wales.

The process of the enclosure of earlier open field systems had begun in various parts of Wales by the late sixteenth century. By 1622, when this survey of the manor of Barry in the Vale of Glamorgan was made by Evans Mouse, virtually all the land had been enclosed (Glamorgan Record Office, D/DF, Manorial).

Opposite: *The droving of cattle to England for fattening and sale became firmly established in late fifteenth-century Wales. A pattern of roads emerged based on the drovers' routes, and these were to have a marked influence on Welsh topography. This bridge at Pont Nant-y-Lladron, Gwynedd, lies close to the modern road between Bala and Ffestiniog (Harry Williams Photographic Libary).*

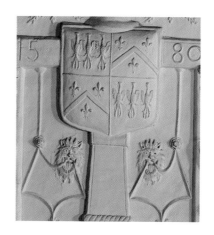

The Act of 'Union' of 1536, modified by
further legislation in 1543, was greatly
to strengthen the position of the
emerging class of Welsh gentry. One of
the rising stars of the Tudor age was the
well-travelled Robert Wynn (d. 1598),
third son of John Wynn of Gwydir. His
arms can be found over the fireplace in
the hall at Plas Mawr, his ambitious
Flemish-style town house in Conwy.

FROM THE 'UNION' TO THE STUART RESTORATION

THE MAKING OF WALES 1536–1660

In the 1530s the English Parliament passed legislation which represented the culmination of developments which had been afoot in Wales for a quarter of a millennium. The legislation would provide a framework for the life of the Welsh people, in matters secular and religious, for the next quarter of a millennium. It had profound implications for the making of Wales. The legal and administrative assimilation of the country by the English state in 1536, and the religious changes initiated by Thomas Cromwell in 1533, culminating in the acceptance of the Thirty-Nine Articles in 1563, had an impact upon every aspect of Welsh life.

The Act of 1536 laid down that the county system established by Edward I in the Principality was to be extended to the March. Seven new counties came into existence and county administration was put into the hands of the Justices of the Peace, men drawn almost exclusively from the emerging gentry class. Wales was to have twenty-seven MPs, fourteen representing the counties and thirteen the boroughs. Central to the assimilation was the abolition of any legal distinction between the Welsh and the English. This meant that the Penal Laws were nullified (though not formally repealed) and that the Law of England would be the only law recognized by the courts of Wales. Thus, in the eyes of the law, the Welsh would henceforth be English. Yet, it would be equally valid to argue — as there was no longer any advantage in boasting of the condition of being English — that henceforth everyone living in Wales was Welsh, a principle which would be built upon in subsequent generations.

The Act of 1536 — modified by that of 1543 — served to define the land of Wales, for (despite the one-time anomalous position of Monmouthshire) Wales has, since the 1530s, been considered to be the territory contained within the thirteen counties. To demarcate the borders of Wales was irrelevant to the legislators of the 1530s, for their intention was to incorporate Wales into England. Yet demarcate it they did. The border thus created did not follow the old line of Offa's Dyke, nor the eastern boundaries of the Welsh dioceses; it excluded districts such as Oswestry and Archenfield, where the Welsh language would continue to be spoken for centuries, districts it would not be wholly fanciful to consider as *Cambria irredenta*.

The Act of 1536 — again modified by that of 1543 — also served to define territories within Wales. Although six of the counties of Wales — Anglesey, Caernarvon, Merioneth, Flint, Cardigan and Carmarthen — date back wholly or partly to the thirteenth century, it was in 1536 that the counties became the primary definition of community beyond the very local. Some of them — Denbighshire, for example — hardly had much geographical coherence, but as

Following the Act of 1536, the county divisions of Wales became the primary definition of community beyond the very local. They were mapped in five different atlases in the first half of the seventeenth century. John Speed's map of Wales, with the county boundaries delineated, was compiled in 1610. In the border at each side, there are miniature depictions of the county towns (The British Library).

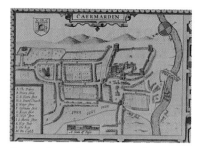

Carmarthen, whose status as the county town of Carmarthenshire was never challenged, was depicted in John Speed's atlas published in 1611 (National Library of Wales).

From the late fifteenth century until 1689, the English border town of Ludlow was the seat of the Council of Wales. In this period, to the extent that Wales as a whole had a single capital it lay here, beyond the country's border.

they were the units for the selection of MPs, the appointment of High Sheriffs and, above all, the judicial and administrative activities of the Justices of the Peace, they rapidly became the focuses of intense loyalty. Cartographers — key figures in the recording of the making of Wales — seized upon the counties as the natural units to depict. Saxton mapped them all in 1579 and they were delineated, each on a separate page, in five different atlases between 1611 and 1645. The counties were also the units for the work of topographers and historians, as the writings of Owen on Pembrokeshire and Merrick and Stradling on Glamorgan testify.

The shiring of Wales meant the designating of thirteen county towns; some of them — Harlech in particular — hardly grew beyond villages, but others gained increased prosperity from their new status. Speed's atlas, published in 1611, contains sketches of shire-halls at Cardiff and Caernarfon and mentions the shire-hall at Denbigh; undoubtedly other halls existed, but no trace of them has survived. By the nineteenth century, nine of the original county towns had proved to be unsuitably located and other centres were chosen. Of the remaining four, the status of Cardiff as county town of Glamorgan was much disputed, but Caernarfon, Carmarthen and Brecon were never challenged as the capitals of their eponymous counties. Those three towns, together with Denbigh, were also the designated seats of the Great Sessions of Wales, a system of courts which lasted until 1830. They were the capitals of the four corners of the country, and, in the hierarchy of Welsh towns, they were the ones with the fullest functions. However, to the extent that Wales as a whole had a capital, it lay beyond the country's border — Ludlow, the one-time *caput* of the marcher lordships of the Mortimers and, from the late fifteenth century until 1689, the seat of the Council of Wales. With its magnificent castle, its splendid church and its delightful townscape, Ludlow cannot but arouse covetousness in a Welsh patriot.

The Reformation, like the incorporation of Wales into England, was an aspect of that intensification of the sovereignty of the English Crown which was the essence of Tudor monarchy. Admittedly, the notion that the coming of the Tudors and the integration of Wales into the legal and administrative system of England meant that anarchy rapidly gave way to effective authority is highly misleading. Yet the growing efficiency of the machinery of government did mean that violence and disorder were coming under increasing control. The belief, already widespread in the late fifteenth century, that the state could provide security, became firmly accepted. Thus the building of fortified dwellings was wholly abandoned, an indication not only of a more peaceable society, but also of an evolutionary tempo much faster than that of most of the rest of Europe.

Increasing security also helped to promote economic growth, which in turn facilitated a marked increase in population. The figures can only be tentative, but it would seem that the number of Wales's inhabitants rose from around 250,000 in 1530 to 360,000 by 1620. Economic growth did not result in the enhancement of the living standards of every section of the expanding population. The period saw dramatic inflation, with the price of ordinary goods rising at least fourfold. The purchasing power of the poorest sections of the community halved and the gulf between the social classes widened greatly. Domestic architecture offers the clearest evidence of the gulf. While the poor continued to occupy temporary hovels — 'dungheaps shaped into cottages', as they were described in the satirical volume *Wallography* — yeomen were able to build increasingly commodious houses and the richer gentry could dwell in palatial surroundings.

As the hundreds of surviving yeomen's houses testify, the years 1530 to 1640 were the era of the great rural rebuilding. Yet that was by no means a Wales-wide phenomenon, for whereas in the Vale of Meifod in northern Montgomeryshire, 'every other house appears seventeenth century or earlier', no house obviously older than 1660 has yet been discovered in the Vale of Aeron in mid Cardiganshire. In the more favoured areas hall-houses were built in great numbers, and increasing wealth permitted the basic hall-house to be progressively modified. The primary modification was the installation of a fireplace and chimney. A great house like Cochwillan in the Ogwen valley had had a fireplace from the beginning, but more modest dwellings had initially been heated by an open fire in the middle of the room. Early fireplaces tended to be erected on the lateral wall or the gable end of the house. This was particularly the practice around Pembroke and St Davids, where the so-called 'Flemish chimneys', with their cylindrical or conical stacks, are so massive that it almost seems that the house has been added to the chimney rather than the chimney to the house. In the north-east, however, it became far more common to place the fireplace across the middle of the hall, either opposite the entry or backing upon the walkway leading from it.

The installation of a chimney had far-reaching implications. If placed internally, it divided the hall into two, thus bringing to an end the concept of a single room as the arena of all household activities. With smoke being drawn up the stack, less ventilation was needed, a development which coincided with

The years from 1530 to 1640 are recognized as a period of great rural rebuilding, with the storeyed house becoming common in most areas. This very simplified map shows the principal regional divisions in the style of houses in Wales. In the west, a style with chimneys on the outer wall predominated. In the eastern part of the country chimneys were more common inside. In the north-east these formed a lobby at the entrance, whereas in the south-east the fireplace backed on to the entry passage (After Smith, in Owen 1989).

Garn at Llanychâr in Pembrokeshire is a good early example of a house with a large fireplace in one of the lateral walls. Here, however, it is a primary feature. The round chimney — a so-called 'Flemish chimney' — is common to the region (Crown Copyright: The Royal Commission on the Ancient and Historical Monuments of Wales).

The four sketches and plans shown here attempt to simplify and summarize the development of the farmhouse in Wales from about 1500 to about 1680 (After Smith, in Owen 1989).

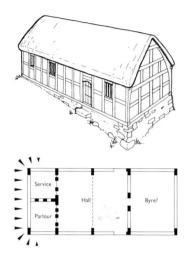

A half-timbered single storey hall-house of about 1500, sited on a hill. There is no formal fireplace, with a hearth probably sited in the floor at the centre of the hall.

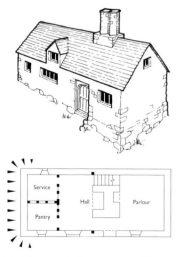

A hall-house rebuilt as a storeyed house about 1560. A fireplace and chimney replace the earlier gable vent arrangement, and the walls are of stone.

a marked increase in the production of window glass. Although smallholders' houses in northern Glamorgan still lacked glass as late as 1820, the dwellings of almost all those of at least modest means had glass windows by 1660, perhaps the greatest single improvement in the standard of living ever to have taken place. An open fireplace in the middle of the floor needs a high headroom for the smoke to disperse, but a house with a chimney can accommodate an upper floor. The consequent doubling of floor space meant that members of even modest families could have bedrooms. By the late sixteenth century, yeomen houses were being built with chimneys and lower and upper floors as integral parts of them, but many dwellings which are now chimneyed, two-storeyed and partitioned are the result of imposing a new arrangement upon an open hall, an imposition which reflected a desire not only for comfort but also for privacy.

The hall-house is encountered on the better land and among the richer farmers. In less favoured districts, long-houses — in which the cowshed and homestead are linked by internal access — predominated. Built of rubble, they have none of the distinction of the hall-houses, and because of their simpler construction they are very difficult to date. Of those that survive, many have medieval origins, but almost all of them have been extensively modified, in particular through the severing of the access between house and beast-house; however, an authentic seventeenth-century long-house in the Hepste valley north of Hirwaun is still inhabited. It is likely also that the outer rooms of some medieval hall-houses housed cattle, but that these were converted into parlours in more prosperous days. Other houses suffered demotion; the fine early cruck hall-house of Tŷ-draw in Llanarmon Mynydd Mawr, for example, eventually became a barn. Many of the constructions intended as outbuildings could vie in quality with hall-houses, as the splendid barn erected at Gellilyfdy in Flintshire in 1586 amply testifies.

While yeomen clung to the two- or three-bay hall-house, the richer gentry were more ambitious, building wings, mullioned windows, stair-wells and elaborate chimney stacks, a style which reached its climax at Pentrehobyn near Mold, a splendid house in the sub-medieval tradition completed in the early seventeenth century. Decades earlier, however, a new style was intruding, for in the later sixteenth century, in the progressive parts of Britain, the classical architecture of the south of Europe was, as Peter Smith has put it, beginning to displace the organic architecture of the north. The Renaissance house brought a revolution in basic plan. There was a novel concern for symmetry; the outward appearance of a building became a prime consideration, with elaborate attention given to the front façade — itself a new concept, for the notion that a house had a front and a back was alien to medieval thinking. A rational analysis of the functional requirements of the interior led to the study of the proportions of the main rooms, to ensuring independent access to each of them, and to the construction of grand staircases. As houses came to have parlours, dining-rooms and libraries, the hall shrank to a mere vestibule. As the designing of houses became more ambitious, it became the work of architects rather than craftsmen, a factor which helped to undermine the vigour of regional building styles.

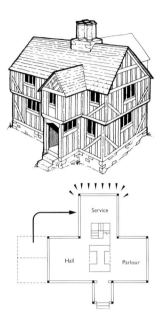

In the half-timbered borderland, this example could date to about 1630. It might be considered an early Renaissance house, with a cruciform or cross-shaped plan, with a porch to the front.

Wales's earliest Renaissance house was Bachegraig, built in the Vale of Clwyd by Richard Clough (d. 1570) three years before his death and now sadly demolished. Inspired by the Flemish Renaissance, it was a cube surmounted by a pyramid roof with two tiers of dormers and crowned by a cupola. At much the same time Clough built Plas Clough near Denbigh, a less innovative building but one which — with its stepped gables — also drew inspiration from the Low Countries. Both houses contained extensive work in brick, which — apart from some of the vaulting at Raglan Castle — had not been used in Wales since Roman times. On occasion, Renaissance features were grafted on to older buildings, most spectacularly at Old Beaupre in the Vale of Glamorgan where in 1600 the 'tower of orders' was added to a fourteenth-century manor house. In addition to Bachegraig and Plas Clough, Welsh houses built under the influence of Renaissance ideas include St Fagans (about 1580), Plas Mawr, Conwy (1595), Plas Teg near Hope (1610), Brynkinalt near Chirk (1612) and Treowen near Monmouth (1627). In most of these buildings, however, pre-Renaissance elements were still a major factor in design, for the full implications of the Renaissance style were not completely absorbed until the later seventeenth century. Plas Mawr is particularly rich in plaster ceilings, an indication of Renaissance liking for surface ornament, as opposed to the exposed, finely-carved roofs preferred by earlier generations, although Plas Mawr has these too, but they were hidden from view as soon as they were completed. A wealth of plasterwork may also be found in the Long Gallery constructed at Powis Castle in the 1590s. Other castles remodelled at least partly in a Renaissance idiom include Carew, where Sir John Perrot (d. 1592) built a suite of five great rooms in the 1580s, and Raglan, where between 1549 and 1628 the earls of Worcester were vigorous builders.

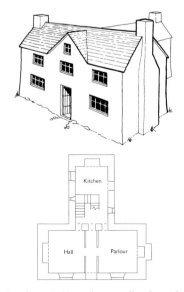

By about 1680, early centrally-planned houses had begun to appear.

Raglan was not only enriched with additional buildings. It was also enhanced by one of the finest gardens ever constructed in Wales. By the death of the fourth earl in 1628, three long walled terraces planted with knot gardens and a large lake containing a series of island parterres adjoined the castle; in addition, there were summer-houses, a bowling green, orchards, hopyards, curved walks and a wealth of statuary. The structure of the garden is still apparent, as are the outlines of sixteenth- and seventeenth-century pleasure grounds at St Donat's, Chirk, Llantrithyd Place, Haroldston and elsewhere. At Troy House near Monmouth the gateway of the walled garden survives, as do the pillars of the entrance to the formal gardens at Old Gwernyfed and the walls of the garden enclosures at Bryn Iorcyn. Some enthusiastic gardeners imported non-indigenous trees to beautify their grounds. Chief among them was the sycamore, which was well-established in Wales by 1660. Thomas Bowen of Trefloyne near Tenby was planting North American conifers in the 1590s and, in the mid-seventeenth century, Thomas Hanmer (1612–78) of Bettisfield was noting his plantations of cypresses, cedars and other exotica. Few if any new species of plants had been introduced into Wales since the Roman era; with the activities of Bowen, Hanmer and others, a process began which would go far to transform the appearance of large areas of Wales.

Raglan Castle had been converted to a veritable palace in the late sixteenth century by William Somerset, third earl of Worcester (d. 1589). Edward, the fourth earl (d. 1628), inherited his father's sophisticated gardens, and went on to add further refinements. These quite wonderful Renaissance gardens, with pools, terraces and parterres, were mapped in 1652 (The National Library of Wales).

The domination of woodland Wales by non-indigenous trees belonged, however, to the future. In the early seventeenth century, there was every indication that the Wales of the future would have no woodland at all. By then, the proportion of the country that was forested had declined to below 10 per cent, although the construction of hedges with their hedgerow trees — as many perhaps as two or three per acre (six per ha) — would have given the landscape a more wooded appearance than the percentage would suggest. Deforestation was caused partly by the decline in the popularity of the chase; there were seventeen known deer parks in sixteenth-century Glamorgan but only three survived into the following century. In addition, many of the great oaks of the borders were felled for shipbuilding; the Rodney Pillar on the Breiddin, erected in 1781, was a belated recognition of the navy's debt to the woodlands of Powys.

Industry, too, took its toll of the forests, although a well-managed woodland can produce charcoal in perpetuity. But not all industrialists were concerned to husband the resources of nature. At Talyfan in Glamorgan, a forest was given over to grazing by sheep in 1596 after the timber had been cut down for smelting, and laments from the Cynon valley indicate the bitterness aroused by ruthless tree-felling there. Other industrial activities were also modifying the landscape. The south Wales coalfield contains a number of bell pits or day holes. They are shallow shafts sunk vertically down to mineral deposits and when no longer being worked they fill up to leave funnel-shaped depressions. In the neighbourhood of Swansea, a port which exported 3,000

In the early seventeenth century, the manor house at Bryn Iorcyn, Flintshire, was enhanced with a series of formal walled garden enclosures, complete with an integral dovecot.

Opposite: *Plas Teg near Hope in Flintshire, built in 1610 by the 'wise, mild, temperate' Sir John Trevor (d. 1630), is one of the most memorable houses in Wales. It is one of several great houses of the period which ushered in the new spirit of the Renaissance.*

tons of coal a year by 1607, mining was transforming an entire landscape, and in the same region the smelting of Cornish copper ores was beginning to cause long-term pollution problems. Leland noted that slate-quarrying was being undertaken in extensive areas of the counties of Caernarvon, Merioneth and Denbigh, and he also described the way in which lead-mining in Flintshire and Cardiganshire was depleting woodland resources.

But it was above all the needs of agriculture which were causing the contraction of the woodlands. The poet Thomas Churchyard praised the Welsh in 1587 for 'They tear up trees and take the roots away... And plough the ground where sturdy oaks did stand'. There was in sixteenth-century Wales, with its rising population, a lust for assarted land. Landlords sought to intensify ownership rights and increase production through large-scale enclosure. Although strip cultivation survived in parts of Cardiganshire, Denbighshire and Glamorgan, almost the whole of lowland Wales had been enclosed by 1640, and thus the enclosure movement which was to loom so large in the English Midlands in the eighteenth century had no Welsh equivalent. Among the gentry, there was a growing interest in improved farming methods, an interest reflected in the lime-kilns which increasingly dotted the landscape. In the uplands, there was much encroachment of the waste and surreptitious enclosure of hill grazings. The flight from the marginal land which followed the demographic crisis of the fourteenth century was being reversed. Between 1530 and 1620, the population of upland parishes increased up to four times more rapidly than did that of lowland parishes, where land available for colonization was in short supply.

It could be argued that the overpopulation apparent in the agrarian economy of 1300 had been replicated in the largely agrarian economy of 1600. Indeed, in 1600 the situation was probably worse, for by then the well-to-do had laid their hands on a higher proportion of the economy's surplus than had their predecessors, three hundred years earlier. Many among the underprivileged believed that they could better themselves by migrating to the towns. As most rural areas were ethnically Welsh, the influx meant that the towns of Wales were, by the early seventeenth century, largely Welsh in speech. Similar developments occurred in rural areas; in the Vale of Glamorgan, where the indigenous population had been swamped by in-migration following the Norman Conquest, migration from the uplands meant that by 1600 the ethnic balance had been reversed. The influx into the towns was a cause of grave concern; in 1603, for example, the Corporation of Swansea expressed its dismay over the town's burgeoning urban proletariat. Although some towns, such as Llandovery, suffered severely because they were no longer the *caput* of a marcher lordship, many doubled in population between 1530 and 1660. Wrexham, with over 3,000 inhabitants, was probably the largest town in Wales by the mid-seventeenth century, but Carmarthen and Brecon were not far behind.

Of the surviving buildings of urban Wales in the period 1530–1660, incomparably the most impressive is Plas Mawr, Conwy. More in keeping with the scale of the Welsh townscape, however, are the half-timbered houses of Ruthin and Beaumaris and the corbelled stone buildings of Tenby and

Plas Mawr in Conwy is undoubtedly the most impressive Elizabethan town house surviving in Wales, and one of the finest in Britain. It was raised in three stages between 1576 and 1585. The third stage involved the construction of a showy gatehouse overlooking High Street.

Pembroke. Presteigne can boast its judges' lodgings and the Radnorshire Arms Hotel, while Llantwit Major has the Swan Inn and a charming town hall. The county hall at Denbigh, mentioned by Speed, was remodelled in 1780, but much of the original work of 1572 is still apparent. Llanidloes has perhaps the most attractive of all of Wales's early civic buildings, the half-timbered market hall built in about 1600. Thirteen endowed grammar schools were established in Wales between 1541 and 1616, but, apart from the old school at Ruthin, little of their original buildings now remain. Riverside towns were eager to acquire stone bridges. Handsome structures had been built across the Dee at

The half-timbered market hall at Llanidloes in Powys was built about 1600 and remains perhaps the most attractive of all Wales's early civic buildings.

The late sixteenth- or early seventeenth-century bridge across the Usk at Crickhowell is particularly graceful. Riverside towns of this period were anxious to improve communications with the construction of such stone bridges.

Holt and Llangollen in about 1500. Other surviving bridges of the sixteenth and early seventeenth centuries include those over the Usk at Brecon and Crickhowell, the Wye at Monmouth and the Conwy at Llanrwst. The last, frequently but almost certainly wrongly attributed to Inigo Jones, is particularly graceful, as is that at Crickhowell, with its segmented arches, its cutwaters and its refuges.

The prosperity of which the urban expansion was a symptom was faltering by the 1620s. Following the poor harvests of 1622–24, death from starvation became commonplace and in 1636–37 the plague returned, as it did again in 1639. Population growth slowed down and then went into reverse, particularly in the 1640s when the Civil War added to the woes caused by nature. The economic dislocation, the looting, the gratuitous cruelty — particularly of the Royalist forces — and the spread of disease which resulted from the war were far more grievous than the deaths in battle. The war had implications for the landscape also. New defences were constructed, such as the bulwarks at Carmarthen, the redoubt at Caerphilly, the reinforcements to the curtain-wall at Chepstow Castle and the artillery bastions at Raglan. In the course of the war, fine houses such as Mathafarn and Caer-gai were destroyed and several towns, Wrexham in particular, suffered greatly. Iconoclastic attacks by Puritans on churches have probably been exaggerated, but Parliamentary soldiers were said to have melted down the organ pipes at Wrexham to make bullets, and the depredations at Llandaff Cathedral were not made good for centuries.

The greatest blow to the Welsh architectural heritage was the decision of the triumphant Parliamentarians to render all castles useless as fortifications. Raglan, the seat of the first marquess of Worcester, Charles I's most ardent supporter, was attacked with crowbars and pickaxes and the great hexagonal tower was undermined, causing two of its sides to collapse. The castles at Aberystwyth and Newcastle Emlyn were blown up, as was the barbican at Pembroke. The great castles of Gwynedd were unroofed; their glass, lead and timber were sold and their staircases were removed, but the decision utterly to demolish the town walls and castle at Caernarfon was not carried out.

Among the activities of the Parliamentarians was the sequestration of the landed possessions of their opponents and of the Church, a policy which could have led to even more sweeping changes in the pattern of landholding that had followed the dissolution of the monasteries. Yet as Cromwell was not vengeful, and as his regime hardly survived him, the Welsh gentry and the Welsh Church did not suffer any large-scale, permanent confiscations. Only one leading Cromwellian built up a substantial estate; he was Philip Jones (d. 1674), whose descendants still live in Fonmon Castle, Wales's oldest continuously inhabited dwelling. Thus the Civil War and the Interregnum, though momentous happenings, did little to interrupt the estate-building activities of the Welsh gentry, activities which allowed them wholly to dominate the life of Wales in the century after 1660.

As a consequence of the Civil War, the decision of triumphant Parliamentarians to render castles useless as fortifications was a great blow to the Welsh architectural heritage. Two sides of the Great Tower at Raglan were brought crashing down following the siege of 1646.

As a close friend of Cromwell, Philip Jones (d. 1674) became a dominant force in south Wales politics in the 1650s. He amassed a considerable estate and with it acquired Fonmon Castle near Barry. A medieval mansion, it was extended in the late seventeenth century and remodelled in the eighteenth century.

'And Peace on Earth to Men of Good Will': A cut-out wooden angel in the private chapel built by Sir Richard Wynn (d. 1674) at Gwydir Uchaf, near Llanrwst, in 1673. Sir Richard's family was among the most distinguished in north Wales, and in economic terms ranked at the aristocratic level.

FROM STUART RESTORATION TO THE INDUSTRIAL REVOLUTION

THE MAKING OF WALES 1660–1780

In 1660, the king and the court, the bishops and the House of Lords were all restored. Yet, although the Restoration appeared to be the triumph of institutions with medieval origins, the true beneficiaries were the greater landowners and the leading figures in the City of London. Henceforth, the king would only be able to rule with the consent of the members of the House of Commons, and they were selected almost exclusively to serve the interests of the landowning élite. In their localities, estate owners were largely free from the interference of the central government and were not seriously threatened by the classes beneath them; for several generations no other class would be able to compete with them in wealth, status and power. In the decades following the Restoration, almost all the landed families adopted strict settlement, a legal arrangement whereby the head of the family, generation after generation, inherited the estate in its entirety. Marriage alliances were the chief factor in ensuring that large estates expanded and that their number contracted. The phenomenon was most marked in the history of the Williams Wynn family of Wynnstay, which, through a series of marriages, united seven estates, thereby creating a landed agglomeration which would eventually embrace some 150,000 acres (60,000ha). The process depended to a large degree upon the emergence of a single heiress, usually the result of the premature death of all her siblings. That could suggest that she came from sickly stock, the explanation, perhaps, of the demographic crisis so marked in Welsh gentry families by 1700 — although the drinking habits of husbands was also probably a factor. As estate accumulation progressed, Welsh heiresses were sufficiently wealthy to attract suitors from beyond Offa's Dyke, a central factor in the Anglicization of the ruling class of Wales.

As estates grew in size, the Welsh ruling class contracted to a few dozen families at most, a development reflected in the repetition of the same names in the lists of Welsh parliamentary representatives. The concentration of land in the hands of the few meant that many houses which had been the seats of gentry families came to have less exalted occupants. The status of the houses at Llwydiarth and Plas y Ward, the centres of estates absorbed into that of Wynnstay, was much demoted. The larger the estate, the more ambitious the building plans of its owner. In the decades after 1660, resident Welsh landowners could construct houses on a scale previously confined to court officials such as John Trevor (d. 1630) of Plas Teg.

The most attractive building erected in Wales in the late seventeenth century was Tredegar House near Newport. Completed by 1680, its appeal lies in its superb symmetry, its lavish ornamentation and its warm brickwork. The pace of building quickened in the eighteenth century, particularly in the north-east, where in the 1720s the halls at Leeswood, Emral, Soughton and Pickhill were completed, all of them in the Baroque tradition. Pickhill Hall, in particular, followed the general contemporary practice of concealing the roof behind a parapet, as did Nanteos, the mansion built near Aberystwyth in 1739. Parapets were also part of the splendid façade of Coldbrook House near Abergavenny (about 1750), of the more severe but excellently proportioned façade at Ynysmaengwyn near Tywyn (1758) and of the remodelled front at Taliaris near Llandeilo (about 1780). By then the revolution in domestic architecture ushered in by the Renaissance was fully appreciated, a

Built for Sir William Morgan (d. 1680), Tredegar House near Newport is the most attractive house erected in Wales in the late seventeenth century. Gardens and parkland which surround the house were also first established during Sir William's time.

Around 1720–60, the Baroque architectural style entered its Rococo phase across much of Europe, though in Britain this found little favour. Examples of playful, scrolled plasterwork do exist, and there is some notable ironwork. A further charming interpretation of the Rococo style can be found in a series of late eighteenth-century carved funeral tablets set up in churches around the Black Mountains. This example by J. Brute can be seen at Patrisio church north of Abergavenny.

Landowners were clearly very keen to beautify their grounds as well as their houses, and there are numerous examples of extensive garden-making across Wales from the century or so after 1660. Garden buildings were to proliferate with this orangery at Margam, built in 1786–90, a late but magnificent example.

development aided by the regular visits of Welsh gentry to Bath and Dublin, and, in the case of the wealthier of them, to the font of the Renaissance in Italy. Building in stone was much assisted by the growing use of explosives in quarries, the reason, perhaps, for the retreat from most of Wales of the tradition of building half-timbered mansions. The tradition lasted longest in Montgomeryshire, but even there it was being abandoned; Plas Newydd, near Carno, erected in 1704, was probably the last 'black-and-white' gentry house to be built in Wales. Brick was used at Tredegar House, Pickhill Hall and Coldbrook House, but, if not burnt at the site as they were at Coldbrook, bricks were more expensive than stone. There are no recorded examples of pre-eighteenth-century brick buildings in south-west or north-west Wales. Elsewhere, building in brick was a foible of the rich. That was to be the case until economies in production came to outweigh the costs of distribution, a situation which did not arise until the development of the canal and railway network.

In many parts of Europe in the eighteenth century, the Baroque style was entering its Rococo phase, marked by elegance and a love for fantastic and asymmetrical decoration. It found little favour in Britain, although Fonmon Castle has a delightful Rococo library. It did, however, appeal to one family of artists, as the superb work of the Davies family of ironsmiths testifies. The gates at Chirk, Leeswood and Erddig are among Wales's greatest treasures; with their whimsical inventiveness, manifested above all at Chirk, they are among Europe's most distinguished examples of late Baroque art. A more naïve, but highly attractive interpretation of Rococo were the carved tablets of Thomas Brute (about 1721–82) and his family; a feature of the churches around the Black Mountains, their unabashed joviality makes for very cheerful funereal monuments.

The Davies gates are evidence of the desire of landowners to beautify their grounds as well as their houses. Further evidence comes from garden-making, an activity much practised by the gentry in the century after 1660. The most magnificent of their efforts are the terraced gardens at Powis Castle, laid out in the 1690s and restored in the twentieth century. Other surviving gardens of broadly the same period include the formal walled enclosures and canal at Erddig near Wrexham, the terraces at Llangedwyn Hall south of Chirk and the yew-hedged garden at Llanmihangel Place in the Vale of Glamorgan. Some of the country's finest erstwhile gardens, such as those at Leeswood, Llannerch and Bettisfield, can now only be traced through forlorn earthworks, overgrown walls and neglected plantations, but a number of handsome avenues survive — walnut at Betws Cedewain, lime at Mostyn and Soughton, oak at Tredegar House, chestnut at Llanfihangel Court north of Abergavenny and Scots pine at Llangybi Castle north of Newport. Garden buildings — orangeries, gazebos, summer houses — proliferated, the most magnificent of them being the orangery at Margam; some 330 feet (100m) in length, it is the largest orangery in the world. The practice of adorning pleasure-grounds with buildings reached its climax at Wynnstay, where the park, bisected by a straight, 1.25-mile (2km) avenue, contains an ornamental dairy, a bath-house and a variety of columns, lodges, towers and gateways.

The avenue at Wynnstay was something of an anachronism, for by the 1770s, when it was laid out, fashionable landscape architects were inveighing against straight lines. The idea that pleasure grounds should be formal, thus contrasting with nature, was being abandoned in favour of the notion that they should be an enhancement of nature, rich in fine clumps of trees, meandering drives, gurgling brooks and sinuous lakes. It is surely significant that the landscaped park should make its earliest appearance in England, the first country in the world where it could convincingly be argued that nature had been brought under control. As nature was no longer a threat, it could surround the house, and the world outside could be separated from the pleasure grounds not by a wall but by a ha-ha.

Gnoll near Neath, where winding paths, cascades and an artificial cave were constructed in the 1740s, is among the earliest of the parks of Wales to be landscaped in the 'Romantic' manner. More magnificent was Piercefield near Chepstow, where the woodland path, now part of the Wye Valley Walk, offered superb views of the Lancaut (Llancewydd) peninsula and the great bend in the river. 'Capability' Brown (1716–83), the leading eighteenth-century landscape architect, redesigned the park at Dinefwr, arranging for the planting of the beech copses which crown the hill above Llandeilo. William Emes, a follower of Brown, was active in the 1760s at Chirk, where he obliterated all formal features, and in the 1770s at Baron Hill, where his plantations framed the view of Snowdon across the Menai Strait. Park-making could involve a major rearrangement of the landscape, with the creation of knolls and escarpments, the diversion of roads, the relocation of farms or even entire villages and the transformation of valleys through damming — work carried out with great panache at Stackpole, west of Tenby. Such activities are proof of the virtually untrammelled power of the greater landlords, and were to be carried out with even more vigour in the half century after 1780.

Piercefield, on the edge of the Wye valley near Chepstow, was set out in the later eighteenth century. It is one of the most successful, dramatic parkland landscapes of this era. This plan of the grounds was published in 1801.

The great landscape park around Chirk Castle owes much of its present day structure to the layout created by William Emes, beginning in 1764.

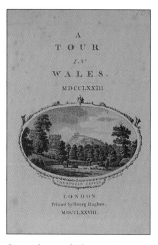

The first volume of Thomas Pennant's (d. 1798) A Tour in Wales was published in 1778, with the second following in 1781. The work was very significant in persuading English intelligentsia that Wales was intellectually interesting (The British Library).

The laying out of parks was an aspect of the Romantic movement, that revolution in sensibility which transformed attitudes towards landscape. While in 1700 sensitive travellers pulled down the blinds of their coach lest they should be pained by the barbarity of mountainous scenery, little more than fifty years later aesthetes were glorying in the wild, the sublime and the Picturesque. Thus, Wales was 'discovered', and by the 1770s the beginnings of a tourist industry could be discerned, an industry which was eventually to dominate much of the Welsh landscape. Mountains changed from supernatural eyesores to natural phenomena, to become eventually marketable commodities.

The north-east, where by 1760 there were five turnpike companies with roads linking the region to the transport system of England, was the first part of Wales to be 'discovered'. In the doggerel, 'The Seven Wonders of Wales', written in the late eighteenth century, all the 'wonders', except for Snowdon, were in the counties of Flint and Denbigh. The north-east was also the home of Thomas Pennant (1726–98), whose *A Tour in Wales* (1778, 1781) was central to the growth among the English intelligentsia of the belief that Wales was intellectually interesting. Appreciation of landscape was fostered by the poets; John Dyer's innovative topographical poem 'Grongar Hill', completed in the 1720s, celebrated the glories of the Tywi valley. Painters promoted the notion of the ideal landscape, with mountain, lake and ruin in splendid asymmetry, images pioneered by Poussin and Claude and continued by the Welsh painter, Richard Wilson (1713–82). Topographical artists, their work reproduced through aquatints and copper engravings, recorded mansions and urban and rural scenes. Moses Griffith of Llŷn executed nearly all the engravings illustrating Pennant's works, and volumes such as those of the two brothers Buck are central to our knowledge of the appearance of eighteenth-century Wales. Equally significant was the work of the cartographers. Ogilby's strip road maps (1675), Collins's coastal charts (1693), and the atlases of Bowen, Kitchin and others, and, above all, the great mass of unpublished estate maps, are fundamental sources for the study of the changing landscape of Wales.

The townscape was changing too, and the eighteenth is the earliest century from which significant quantities of the buildings of urban Wales survive. Welsh towns were still very small; in the mid-eighteenth century, about a fifth of the population was urban, a proportion only marginally higher than that of the High Middle Ages. The number of towns with more than 1,500 inhabitants probably did not exceed a dozen, for the chief urban centres of the various regions of Wales lay outside the country, at Bristol, Shrewsbury, Chester and Dublin. Most of the towns of Wales existed primarily to serve the agricultural communities surrounding them, although industry was helping to swell the populations of Swansea and Wrexham, and to make towns of hitherto inconsiderable villages, as at Holywell and Pontypool. With their mouldering castles and collapsing walls and gates, many Welsh towns could appear to be in an advanced state of dilapidation; with their piles of dung and excrement, tanning yards, rotting vegetables and carcasses, and absence of drains and pavements they could be highly insalubrious. Yet grossly insanitary neighbourhoods could lie cheek by jowl with commodious and immaculate housing, for the contrast between rich and poor was more stark in the towns than in the countryside.

The commodious houses belonged in the main to professional men, for the eighteenth century saw a marked expansion in middle-class vocations. Lawyers, doctors, bankers, merchants, land agents, salaried government officers and master mariners rose in numbers and status. They built town houses, as did the landed gentry in local capitals such as Brecon and Carmarthen. In those towns which later expanded vastly almost all such houses have been swept away; it is therefore the towns which stagnated, or

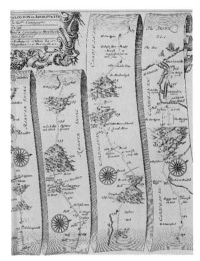

John Ogilby's 'strip road maps', published in his Britannia *of 1675, are one of the sources central to our knowledge of the appearance of Wales in the late seventeenth century (The British Library).*

In the mid to late eighteenth century, Swansea was one of the few towns in Wales with more than 1,500 inhabitants. It is estimated that its population around 1760 was about 3,000. This engraving of the castle and town was published by the brothers Samuel and Nathaniel Buck in 1741 (National Library of Wales).

enjoyed only modest growth, which offer evidence of eighteenth-century urban development. Monmouth, Abergavenny, Brecon, Cowbridge, Carmarthen, Tenby, Haverfordwest, Builth, Welshpool, Llanfyllin, Denbigh, Conwy and Beaumaris all have handsome streets of the period, although some eighteenth-century houses are now concealed beneath later façades. Above all, there is Montgomery, where the town hall of 1748 nestles in a mesh of streets rich in eighteenth-century cornices, doorcases, fanlights, gables, dormer windows, octagonal-fronted bows and a wealth of other undisturbed delights.

By the eighteenth century, Renaissance ideals had filtered down to local builders. Middle-class houses gradually began to display scaled-down aspects of the classical idiom, with central doorways, symmetrically placed windows and emphasized quoins and keystones. The sash window, introduced to Britain from the Netherlands in 1685, rapidly replaced casements in all but the smallest houses. They became a hallmark of the buildings erected in the territories of the British Crown, a contrast with the casement windows preferred in most of mainland Europe. A sash window is a tall oblong opening with the glazing pattern broken by a dominant horizontal bar; a casement window is usually a wide oblong opening with a dominant vertical bar. The difference goes far to explain why the impact of a Welsh or an English street scene differs from that made by a street scene in France or Germany.

The urge to build was, by the eighteenth century, expressing itself almost totally in secular terms. In the High Middle Ages, up to half the investment in building was motivated by religion, but in the century after 1660 the proportion was very small indeed. The Salusburys built a private chapel at Rug in 1637, as did the Wynns at Gwydir Uchaf in 1673, buildings prized as rare examples of Anglican places of worship retaining the liturgical arrangements of seventeenth-century high churchmanship. Such activity was unusual,

Opposite: The handsome little border town of Montgomery, with its town hall of 1748, is one of the most delightful Georgian architectural feasts in Wales.

The Wynn family chapel at Gwydir Uchaf near Llanrwst is a rare example of an Anglican place of worship retaining elements of seventeenth-century high church liturgical arrangements.

Many churches in Wales fell into decay in the eighteenth century, and none was more significant than Llandaff Cathedral. Much of the structure became ruinous, with roofs collapsing. In 1750, a classical temple was raised in the choir and nave, though all traces of this are now gone. The form of John Wood's temple can be seen in this engraving of 1846 (National Museum & Gallery Cardiff).

for less than a dozen churches were built in Wales between 1660 and 1770. The finest of them is St Deiniol, Worthenbury, south-east of Wrexham (1736–39), with its semi-circular apse and its Rococo plasterwork. Some ruinous churches — St Myllin, Llanfyllin, for example, and St Mary's, Monmouth — were rebuilt, but many were left to decay further, thus bequeathing problems to the church reformers of the nineteenth century. Llandaff Cathedral became a ruin; the south-west tower collapsed and the roof of the nave fell in, and all that was done was to erect in 1750 a classical temple — 'a much more serious piece of architecture', as John Newman has put it, 'than later critics imagined'. Landowners preferred to spend on funereal monuments, elaborate, sophisticated memorials such as that to the Myddletons at St Mary's, Chirk.

While the Anglicans were building few places of worship, Christians of other traditions were launching a remarkable building campaign. The Toleration Act of 1689 permitted Protestant, Trinitarian Dissenters to worship freely, provided they licensed their meeting-houses. Some of the founders of Welsh Dissent had built places of worship — the remains of that of Wales's earliest Baptist congregation (1649) may be seen at Ilston in Gower — but during the era of persecution services were generally held in the open air or even in caves. After 1689, purpose-built chapels could be erected. Some congregations did not choose, or did not have the resources, to do so. Private houses remained the centres of many dissenting churches, and other congregations met in outbuildings; until 1749, the Independents of Llanbrynmair worshipped at a lean-to conventicle on the farm of Tŷ Mawr. In more prosperous areas — Abergavenny and Llanwenarth, for example — the opportunity to build a chapel was immediately seized. The investment in construction was not great; a chapel usually cost between £60 and £100, although £252 was spent on Trosnant Baptist chapel, built near Pontypool in 1779.

The simplest of the early meeting-houses were those of the Quakers. Dolobran, south of Llanfyllin, where all the fittings have been carried off to Philadelphia, was built in 1700 by the Lloyd family, founders of Lloyds Bank; it is movingly austere, as is Pales, east of Llandrindod. Among the Independents and the Baptists, with their emphasis upon preaching, meeting-houses were designed to ensure that the largest possible number were able to hear the preacher. Where Nonconformity flourished, chapels were almost invariably rebuilt and thus, even in the heartlands of early Dissent, the chapels tend to be nineteenth-century structures. The earliest chapels are most numerous in regions such as Radnorshire, where the population and the dissenting tradition stagnated. Early chapels were usually oblong boxes, with the one or two entrances on the long wall and the pulpit on the opposite long wall. Maesyronnen, west of Hay, a cruck-roofed building converted into a chapel at the end of the 1690s, is the earliest surviving example, and it is there, above all, that the quintessence of early Welsh Nonconformity may be experienced.

In the mid-eighteenth century, the number of Nonconformists in Wales was very small, but by then a movement had been launched which would eventually greatly increase the proportion of chapel-goers among the inhabitants of Wales. The Methodist Revival, which in Wales took a Calvinist form in contrast with the Arminian tendencies of the Wesleyanism of England, originally aimed at revitalizing the established Church. Its leaders had no intention of creating a new denomination, or, initially at least, of building meeting-houses. Yet the Calvinistic Methodists became a denomination in 1811 and long before that they found that they needed their own places of worship. In 1742, seven years after the conversion of Howel Harris (1714–73), the most dynamic of the leaders of the Revival, the members of the congregation at Groeswen near Caerphilly built themselves a meeting-house.

In 1696–97, the Independents converted an early cruck-roofed building at Maesyronnen, near Hay on Wye, to serve as a new chapel. The building is utterly simple in appearance and is the place to experience the quintessence of early Welsh Nonconformity.

The oldest surviving Methodist place of worship in Wales can be found at Aberthin near Cowbridge. The first chapel was built in 1749 and was replaced in 1780 by the building which now serves as the village hall.

It was Wales's first Methodist place of worship, but its congregation defected to the Independents in 1745. The second to be built — that at Aberthin near Cowbridge — remained in the possession of the Methodists. A low, whitewashed building with a long-wall entrance flanked by two windows, it was the first-fruit of a building programme which, over the following one hundred and fifty years, would endow Wales with hundreds of Methodist chapels. In style, the great majority of later chapels derive, however distantly, from the Renaissance hall-nave. Ironically, Howel Harris himself preferred a different tradition; the Gothick premises he built for his 'commune' at Trefeca were broadly contemporary with the celebrated use of that style by Horace Walpole at Strawberry Hill.

Dissent and Methodism found their most ardent supporters among the 'middling sort of people', the substantial farmers of the countryside and the aspiring lower middle class of the towns. The growing allegiance to such religious movements indicates that the membership of those social groupings was increasing, evidence that the economy of Wales was becoming more prosperous and diversified. That economy could sustain more people, although many of the additional mouths were inadequately fed. It would seem that Wales's inhabitants increased in number from 360,000 in 1660 to 530,000 by 1780. The increase was not a smooth upward progress. A run of bad harvests in the 1690s — the era of the 'Little Ice Age' — resulted in a severe crisis of subsistence; child deaths at Wrexham trebled and local dearth in the hill country of Montgomeryshire scythed down the more vulnerable. Smallpox became virulent, carrying off up to a quarter of the population of Penmachno in 1705–06; other diseases, too, were lethal, the typhus epidemic of 1727–31 causing great mortality. Yet the evidence of the parish registers — admittedly flawed — suggests that in most years after about 1710, births exceeded deaths by a significant margin, and that the excess became more marked after 1750; indeed, it would seem that between 1750 and 1780 the Welsh population was increasing at the rate of 2.75 per cent per decade.

The increase had a marked impact upon the landscape. Settlement on marginal mountainous land, apparent before 1660, became more extensive as the eighteenth century advanced. Transhumance, a long-declining practice, became extinct as high-altitude holdings became independent farms. Vast lengths of dry stone walls were constructed; a feature of much of the Welsh uplands, they represent, perhaps, the most laborious activity ever undertaken by the makers of Wales. Much of the land brought into cultivation was the waste land of Crown manors, for usurping the property of the Crown was one of the primary undertakings of eighteenth-century Welsh landowners. Many areas were enclosed through informal agreement. In 1760, however, unenclosed land north of Welshpool became the subject of an Enclosure Act; by 1780 another five acts had been passed, but, in that year, a quarter of the land of Wales was still unenclosed, for the great boom in enclosure acts occurred in the following three decades. While legislators were changing the pattern of ownership in the uplands, it was the peasantry who were the main agents in changing their appearance. There was a widely, but erroneously, held belief that anyone who could build in one night a cottage on the waste became

the owner of it. Thus the *tai unnos* constructed by the homeless and the destitute became necklaces around the boundaries of the *ffriddoedd* (the upland grazing lands). The impact upon the landscape aroused widespread comment. On the slopes of the Brecon Beacons, for example, 'it seemed as if an Irish estate had been transferred and filled in as a patchwork among the Welsh mountains'.

In the lowlands too the rising population and the increasing pace of economic development were modifying the landscape. Progressive landowners were eager to reorganize their holdings. The arable strips inherited from medieval forms of tenure still existed, as the numerous references to quillets indicate, but the urge to create consolidated farms and to construct hedges was great. The landscape characteristic of lowland Wales — small fields with meandering hedges — was emerging, a marked contrast with the 'new' landscape of Midland England, with its large fields and straight hedges.

As the eighteenth century progressed, settlement on marginal mountainous land became more extensive. High altitude holdings became independent farms, with vast lengths of dry stone walls constructed across the landscape. Such walls can be seen in the distance in this dramatic scenery in Snowdonia.

Crooked hedges were preferred, for they were believed to provide better shelter for cattle. Fields could be very small indeed; in Carmarthenshire it was not unusual for there to be fifteen to twenty on a farm of 50 to 60 acres (20 to 24ha), and hedges could constitute up to 10 per cent of the area of a holding. As early as the 1730s, some Welsh landowners were practising crop rotation and planting clover, hops, potatoes and turnips, thus adding new elements to the rural scene. The more progressive among them were anxious to have firmer control over the activities of their tenants. 'Every field will be kept to the culture I dictate', declared the enthusiastic improver Philip Yorke (d. 1804), the owner of the Erddig estate. This often involved the replacement of the traditional life leases with annual leases, a change with implications for rural housing. With life-leaseholders, the farmhouse and its outbuildings were generally the responsibility of the tenant, who built and repaired in the

Progressive landlords of the eighteenth century were eager to reorganize their holdings. Small fields with meandering hedges was the landscape characteristic of lowland Wales. This fieldscape with hedgerows is in the hills of mid Wales, near Llanidloes in Powys.

tradition of the locality. With annual leases, they were the responsibility of the landowner, who might introduce new building practices and materials. Yet too much should not be claimed. The linking of estate with estate had led to an increase in the number of absentee landlords, many of whom had only a tenuous relationship with their tenants; the tenants themselves, profoundly conservative and lacking in capital, were often deeply resistant to any pressures for change.

With the quickening of economic growth, the proportion of the inhabitants of Wales not wholly dependent upon agriculture for their livelihood increased. The woollen industry moved into its proto-industrial phase. By the 1770s, there were fifteen fulling mills around Dolgellau and, on many farms, outbuildings were adapted as *tai gwŷdd* (loom houses). More significant as an indicator of the future was the growth in the mining and metallurgical industries. In 1693, legal action over the lead mine at Esgair-hir in Cardiganshire led to the recognition that base metal ores were the property of the owners of the land from which they were extracted, a decision central to the readiness of landowners to encourage mining. Cardiganshire, where in the 1750s 2,000 lead miners were tunnelling and creating spoil-heaps, was, declared Lewis Morris, 'the richest county I ever saw'. Lead mining had its periods of prosperity in Flintshire too, where coal mining and copper smelting also flourished. Dr Johnson, visiting Holywell in 1774, counted nineteen different works within 2 miles (3.2km) of St Winifred's Well; indeed, so varied were the early enterprises at Holywell that the Greenfield valley below the town is a veritable open-air museum of industrial archaeology. Neath was even more important as a centre for smelting non-ferrous ores, and there in the 1710s the progressive entrepreneur, Humphrey Mackworth (d. 1727), built the first tramways in Wales, an activity which would absorb much of the energies of industrialists in subsequent decades. Neath, however, was to yield first place to Swansea; by the 1750s, Swansea was the source of half the smelted copper in Britain, much to the distress of those who would have preferred their town to earn a genteel reputation as a spa and watering-place. Smelting poisoned the land around the works; successful reclamation schemes were launched in the 1960s, but they made no provision for the retention of historic copper-smelting plants. The White Rock Industrial Archaeology Park does, however, contain some evidence of the eighteenth-century works. River quays of the 1770s also survive and slag shaped into bricks is much in evidence in buildings around Swansea.

Initially, at least, iron-smelting did not expand as rapidly as did the smelting of other ores. Abraham Darby had discovered in 1709 that iron could be smelted with coked coal, but as charcoal was preferred, at least until the mid-eighteenth century, iron-making continued to be located sporadically and close to sources of coppice wood. From the 1730s onwards, however, ironmasters at Bersham, near Wrexham, at Pontypool and above all at Merthyr Tydfil were establishing furnaces which were eventually to transform large tracts of Wales. The impact upon the landscape of mid-eighteenth-century iron-making may best be appreciated at Bersham, where the Clywedog valley is rich in industrial monuments.

The eighteenth-century expansion of the mining and metallurgical industries was a significant indicator of future economic growth. At Esgair-hir in Cardiganshire, seen here from the air, legal action over the lead mine in 1693 led to the recognition that base metal ores were the property of the owner of the land from which they were extracted. Thereafter, landowners were ready to encourage mining. By the 1750s, 2,000 lead miners were at work in Cardiganshire (Crown Copyright: The Royal Commission on the Ancient and Historical Monuments of Wales).

By the 1750s, Swansea had become a major centre for the smelting of non-ferrous ores. The lower part of the Swansea valley was the source of half the smelted copper in Britain, and the area was to retain its importance in this respect for some considerable time. This engraving of 1810 shows the Hafod copper works on the Tawe (Welsh Industrial and Maritime Museum).

The growth of smelting with coke meant that coal-mining, which had originally been an independent industry concerned largely with exports, became, for a period at least, subordinate to metal-working, and serving mainly a home market. Mackworth was one of the coal industry's pioneers; his workings at Neath were not the traditional shallow holes, for he had mines up to 360 feet (110m) deep, with engines to raise coal and water from the base of the shafts. Increasing demand and improving techniques caused coal production in Wales to increase from 220,000 tons in 1750 to 760,000 tons in 1775. Although the proportion of the output exported declined, its tonnage did not. Swansea exported 8,694 tons of coal in 1710 and 64,502 tons in 1780.

The increasing pace of economic activity was both a cause and a result of improved transport. Before the coming of the turnpike trusts in the mid-eighteenth century, the roads of Wales were uniformly appalling. A traveller in Monmouthshire drowned in a pothole in the 1690s; it must have been of considerable depth, for he was on horseback at the time! The five bills relating to turnpikes in the north-east passed by 1760 had, by 1780, been supple-

The turnpike companies of the eighteenth century built new roads and improved existing ones. They recouped their expenditure through levying tolls. Toll-houses were to become a new feature of the landscape. This example survives at Abergavenny.

mented by thirty-five acts relating to all the regions of Wales. The turnpike companies built new roads or improved existing ones, recouping their expenditure through levying tolls. Road-building had wide-ranging landscape implications. The post road to Holyhead was improved in the 1770s, opening up much wild country and leading to the erection of coaching inns and toll-houses. Cernioge, high on the Denbigh Moors, was a well-known posting-house, and there are attractive toll-houses at Pentrefoelas, Llangollen and Chirk. Better roads encouraged tourism and led to the rise of spas and watering-places. By the 1750s, Llandrindod had a hundred-bed hotel with in-house shops, ballrooms, concert rooms and billiard rooms. Turnpike companies were obliged in 1773 to erect milestones, and those that survive are a delightful feature of the landscape.

The expanding road network increased the demand for bridges. In mid Wales, the Usk, the Wye and the Severn were all repeatedly and handsomely bridged, work which perhaps can be best appreciated at Llandrinio, where in 1775 the Severn was spanned by a three-arched bridge of yellow sandstone. The most remarkable bridge of eighteenth-century Wales is at Pontypridd, where in 1756 William Edwards, a stonemason of Eglwysilan, succeeded in spanning the Taff with a single arch; 150 feet (46m) across, it was at the time the widest stone arch in Europe and was much featured in paintings and engravings. Edwards built at least another seven bridges; that at Dolauhirion, north of Llandovery, is virtually in its original state and it has all the grace of its prototype at Pontypridd.

There was investment in water as well as land transport, for the expansion of sea-borne trade was one of the leading features of the eighteenth-century Welsh economy. Mackworth constructed a small dock at Neath in about 1720. By 1780, the 3 navigable miles (4.8km) of the river Tawe were lined with wharfs, coal banks and quays, and Swansea was much agitated by the need to deepen the river and to remove the bar at its mouth. The town quay at Cardiff was rebuilt in 1760 and similar work was being undertaken along the Dee estuary at Flint, Greenfield, Mostyn and Ffynnongroyw. There was activity at Holyhead, Beaumaris, Bangor, Barmouth, Cardigan and Haverfordwest, with the construction of warehouses and the lengthening and strengthening of quays. Lighthouses were built at St Ann's Head at the opening of the Milford Haven, on Flatholm and at Point of Ayr, but perhaps the most intriguing constructions produced by the expanding sea trade were the watchtowers built along the north Wales coast to give warning of pirate raids.

Yet, as with agricultural improvements, too much should not be claimed. In 1780, Welsh ports were still almost wholly underdeveloped and the country's roads still grossly inadequate. Despite increasing industrial development, those employed in agriculture were the majority in almost all the hundreds of Wales. Although mining in particular had greatly changed the appearance of some localities of Wales, those localities were small islands in an overwhelmingly rural environment. But this situation was not destined to endure, for in the decades after 1780 the activities of the makers of Wales brought about a transformation on a wholly unprecedented scale.

The expanding road network of the eighteenth century led to an increased demand for bridges. In 1756, William Edwards succeeded in spanning the Taff at Pontypridd with a single-arched bridge — the widest stone arch in Europe at the time. It was to feature in many engravings, as in this example by S. Alken from an original by J. Smith (National Museum & Gallery Cardiff).

The construction of lighthouses was one reflection of the expansion of sea-borne trade in the late eighteenth century. Point of Ayr lighthouse was first built in 1777, designed by Joseph Turner.

THE FIRST INDUSTRIAL ERA

THE MAKING OF WALES 1780–1850

The decades between 1780 and 1850 were the era of the remaking of Wales. In seventy years the population more than doubled from 530,000 to 1,189,000, and the proportion employed in agriculture declined to a third. The islands of industry perceptible in 1780 were linked up to become industrial belts, particularly in an arc along the upper edge of the south Wales coalfield. By 1851, there were eighteen towns in Wales with populations of more than 5,000, a figure not reached by any of the towns of Wales in 1780. The largest of them was Merthyr Tydfil, the home of 46,378 people by 1851, and it was there above all that the new Wales in the making was most apparent. Merthyr, and the rest of the industrial communities straddling the northern boundaries of Glamorgan and Monmouthshire, developed to serve the iron industry, which was becoming dominated by a few leviathans. In the early eighteenth century, Wales's largest iron manufactory, that of the Hanbury family at Pontypool, produced 400 tons of iron a year; by the 1840s Dowlais, the largest of Merthyr's four major iron companies, was producing 75,000 tons a year. Meanwhile, the belt of earlier industrial development, stretching from Llanelli to Neath, continued to be an important iron and coal producing region. By the mid nineteenth century, this area dominated world trade in tinplate and copper.

The scale of this industrial development, and the size of its units of production, went far to determine the nature of the communities brought into existence to serve it. In the heads of the valleys region of south Wales an equal, if not more important factor, was the upland location of the centres of iron-making. Merthyr is 750 feet (230m) above sea level, while Beaufort and Brynmawr are at altitudes exceeding 1,300 feet (400m). The early industrial communities sprang up in areas which were previously virtually uninhabited, and therefore they could not draw upon pre-industrial civic and architectural traditions. Housing, urban amenities and transport facilities had to conform to the contours, thus producing in the south Wales coalfield a townscape unique in character.

Early industrialists were proud of their undertakings and liked to have them in full view. Thus Cyfarthfa Castle (1825), a chunky, crenellated pile, overlooked the works of the Crawshay family, and at Dowlais, Penydarren, Nant-y-glo and elsewhere, the owner's grand house offered a prospect of his works. As in many areas the houses of the workers contrasted painfully with those of the ironmasters. By the later nineteenth century, when most of the hillside terraces so characteristic of the south Wales coalfield were built, by-laws and public health considerations had ensured that some basic standards were observed. In the period 1780 to 1850, however, lack of regulation and the need to house a growing influx of workers quickly and cheaply meant the large-scale construction of dwellings that soon proved inadequate. Most of them have now been swept away, but until recently they survived in large numbers, especially in Merthyr Tydfil and the other heads of the valleys towns. The most primitive were the one-room-and-loft dwellings of Bunkers Row, built at Blaenavon in about 1789 and demolished in 1972. Somewhat larger are the row of two-roomed cottages which survives as an office at Jones Court in Cardiff. From 1810 to 1825 the Crawshays favoured a three-roomed house, with the extra room at the back covered by a 'catslide' roof, the layout of the Rhydycar row rebuilt at the Museum of Welsh Life, St Fagans. At Blaenavon, too, many three-room houses were built and similar houses are preserved in modernized form at Forge Row, Cwmafon. The steep hillsides of

Merthyr Tydfil was the greatest iron town of Wales, and had expanded to become the home of 46,378 people by 1851. There were four major iron companies. This painting of 1840 by G. Childs shows the furnace area at the Dowlais works (Welsh Industrial and Maritime Museum).

The Crawshay 'feudal stronghold' of Cyfarthfa Castle (1825) was sited to overlook the family's ironworks.

The need to house the workers for the booming iron industry led to the large-scale construction of dwellings. Upper New Rank was one of the many rows of three-room houses built by the Blaenavon Ironworks proprietors between 1817 and 1830, and all were demolished by 1973. On the ground floor each had a living room with fireplace, a small unheated bedroom, and a larder. There was a big sleeping room above, open to the underside of the roof, with a small front window at floor level near a corner of the room (Jeremy Lowe).

the coalfield offered sites for 'dual' rows, one built over another, as occurred at Nant-y-glo about 1794. The lower houses were of one storey, built 'back-to-earth' and entered from the downhill side; the two-storey upper houses had their doors at ground level on the uphill side. Examples of the more spacious houses of skilled workers may be seen at Blaenavon, where Stack Square and Engine Row, built between 1789 and 1792, have been restored. Some industrialists were more ambitious in their housing schemes. Butetown (y Drenewydd), built in the 1820s, and now admirably refurbished, has fine symmetrical façades and overhanging roofs; a scaled-down version of Butetown — Chapel Row at Blaenavon — was demolished in the 1970s, a fate which also overtook the remarkable Triangle built in the 1840s by the Plymouth Ironworks at Pentrebach.

Of the ironworks themselves, little that was constructed before 1850 can be traced on the sites of most major undertakings, for in the later nineteenth century leading ironmasters invested heavily in new processes. Furthermore,

The Triangle at Pentrebach, Merthyr Tydfil, was built between 1839 and 1844 for the Plymouth Ironworks to house its workers. The layout was due mainly to the boundaries of the land available. The houses were well built and had four rooms. They were typical in design for their date, but above average size, maybe to reward workers who had not taken part in the Chartist uprising of 1839. There were no internal services; privies, each shared by up to ten households, were built over a stream behind the row (Jeremy Lowe).

some of the iron towns — Merthyr in particular — have been remarkably negligent towards their industrial heritage. Elsewhere evidence is more plentiful. On the site of the Neath Abbey Ironworks, there are two superb furnaces of 1793, among the tallest masonry furnaces ever constructed. At Blaenavon the main enterprise was resited in the 1850s and the original works are being restored. The cast-houses, the five blast furnaces and the calcining kilns form a remarkable group, overtopped by the magnificent water-balance tower. Over the mountain lay the forges of Garnddyrys, linked to Blaenavon by a 1.5-mile (2.5km) tunnel; opened in about 1815, it was the longest through tunnel on any railway of its era. Garnddyrys, with its leering mass of slag, is a hugely evocative place. At Merthyr, too, early evidence is not wholly absent: Watkin George's early iron canal bridge, built in the 1790s and dismantled in 1970, has been re-erected at Chapel Row; the remains of Cyfarthfa Ironworks are due to be restored, while nearby lies the already admirably restored engine-house at Ynysfach (1836). Treforest offers an even more impressive example of the activities of the Crawshay family; there, the rolling mill, smithy and tinning house (1834–35) provide unrivalled evidence of the tinplate industries of nineteenth-century Wales.

Essential to the prosperity of the ironworks of the hill country was an effective way of conveying their output to the ports. The matter was addressed between 1790 and 1812 when a number of canals were built, including the four linking the hill country with the ports of Swansea, Neath, Cardiff and Newport. Canal-building was a major enterprise; aqueducts, tunnels, feeders and bridges had to be constructed and fifty-one locks were needed on the 25-mile (41km) canal linking Merthyr with Cardiff. The canals of the coalfield have suffered many indignities; made redundant by the coming of railways, their vulnerability to subsidence, their lack of links with a wider network and their numerous locks have caused them to be largely abandoned, although attractive stretches of the Neath Canal have been restored, and the fine series of locks on the Monmouthshire Canal north of Newport remains an impressive monument.

Two superb furnaces of 1793 — among the tallest masonry examples ever constructed — survive at the site of the Neath Abbey Ironworks.

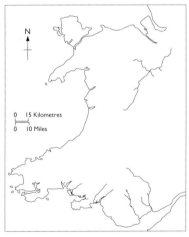

Canals built in Wales by about 1840.

An effective way of conveying the output of their works to the ports was essential to the ironmasters of the hill country. Canals were an early answer, and a number of these waterways were built between 1790 and 1812. The Glamorganshire Canal was begun in the 1790s, and included fifty-one locks on its passage between Merthyr and Cardiff. This early photograph shows a stretch with a pair of locks at Pontypridd (Welsh Industrial and Maritime Museum).

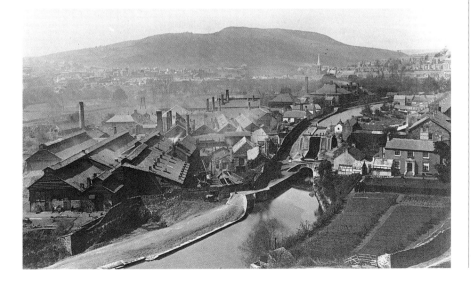

The canal and railway building which linked the iron-making of the uplands to the ports in turn led to the expansion of dock facilities. The sole financier behind the construction of Cardiff's West Bute Dock was John, second marquess of Bute (d. 1848). When it was opened in 1839, the dock was acclaimed as the largest masonry example in the world. Its construction was central to the eventual emergence of Cardiff as the greatest urban centre in Wales. This early photograph shows schooners and brigs at the south end of the dock (Welsh Industrial and Maritime Museum).

Canal construction went hand in hand with the building of tramroads — the horse-worked railways of the pre-locomotion age. Although expenditure on canals was greater, tramroad building was a more widespread activity; about 1,800 miles (2,880km) of tramroads were built within the south Wales coalfield, compared with 160 miles (256km) of canals. Wales has uniquely rich associations with early railway history. Among many dramatic tramways is the Llanfoist incline, where it is possible to find stone sleepers and grooves cut by hauling ropes. The world's first regular railway passenger service was on the Oystermouth Railway at Swansea in 1807. The earliest known iron aqueduct, which also carried a tramroad, is Pantycafnau at Merthyr Tydfil, built by Watkin George in 1793 to serve the Cyfarthfa Ironworks. The first ever use of a steam locomotive to haul a load on a railway was made on the Penydarren Tramroad near Merthyr by Richard Trevithick (d. 1833) in 1804.

Trevithick's experiment was the harbinger of the age of the locomotive. By 1850, the railway age had arrived. Wales's first railway line built specifically for locomotives was that from Llanelli to Pontarddulais, opened in 1839. It was followed in 1841 by the Taff Vale Railway linking Merthyr with Cardiff, the inauguration of the south Wales coalfield's second industrial revolution. In the following nine years, at least twenty bills relating to railway development within the coalfield were passed, and by 1850 the implications of locomotion, for society, for the economy, and for the landscape, were apparent. Canal and railway building led to the expansion of dock facilities. The Town Dock at Newport was opened in 1842 and floating harbours and improved wharfs were constructed at Swansea, Neath, Llanelli and Burry Port. Above all, Cardiff acquired the West Bute Dock, acclaimed on its opening in 1839 as the largest masonry dock in the world; financed solely by the marquess of Bute, its construction was central to the eventual emergence of Cardiff as the largest urban centre in Wales.

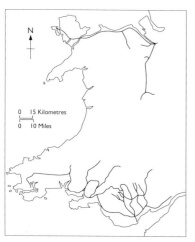

Railways built in Wales between 1839 and 1860.

So far, the industrial impact of the economic growth of the period 1780–1850 has been considered solely in the context of the south Wales coalfield — and justifiably so, for the economy of which Merthyr was the crucible grew until it sustained well over half the population of Wales. But, in many respects, economic growth had a more spectacular impact upon the landscape in other parts of Wales. The canals of the south Wales coalfield, although more significant economically, do not have the visual appeal of other Welsh canals — the Brecknock and Abergavenny (1799, 1812), the navigable feeder of the Ellesmere Canal, starting at Llandysilio near Llangollen (1808) and the Montgomeryshire Canal (1819). All are delectable, and the canal to Llandysilio includes two marvels — Telford and Jessop's aqueducts at Chirk and Froncysyllte. The latter, 'the stream in the sky', is the most astounding achievement of the canal age; an iron trough, 1,020 feet (310m) long, 130 feet (40m) above the ground and held up by nineteen piers, it was hailed by Sir Walter Scott as 'the finest work of art I have ever seen'. Telford was also the engineer of the schemes to improve the coast route between Chester and Bangor and to reconstruct the Holyhead road. As part of the former work he designed the Conwy suspension bridge (1826), which with its crenellated towers superbly complements the castle. As part of the latter, he was responsible for the Menai Bridge (1819–26); its elegance and unprecedented span of 585 feet (178m) won such fame that, in distant Russia, the poet Pushkin sang its praises.

The Conwy suspension bridge, opened in 1826, was designed by Thomas Telford (d. 1834) as part of a general scheme to improve the coast route between Chester and Bangor.

Telford and Jessop's ten-arch aqueduct of 1796–1801 at Chirk was built for the Ellesmere Canal. The viaduct by Henry Robertson was raised almost fifty years later, in 1846–48, for the Shrewsbury and Chester Railway. Together they present a spectacle of almost Roman grandeur.

Penybryn, Cwmystwyth, consisted of two short blocks each of three two-room houses, with an open loft over the smaller room much like rural cottages of the day. They were built about 1835 and demolished about 1979 (Jeremy Lowe).

Other features, too, prove that industry could leave as visible a mark in other parts of Wales as it did in the south Wales coalfield. The scarred landscape at Minera, the massive bleach works at Lleweni, the neo-gothic lime-kilns at Llandybie, the extensive lead mines of Cwmsymlog and Cwmystwyth, the numerous small woollen mills of Cardiganshire, the brick pits at Buckley, and the Dyfi Furnace near Machynlleth all testify to the quickening pace of economic growth. The excavation of the great hole at the Penrhyn slate quarry was well under way by 1850, as was the creation of the vast caverns at Blaenau Ffestiniog. Of all the memorials to nineteenth-century Welsh industry, the most spectacular is in Anglesey. Copper-ore mining on Mynydd Parys south of Amlwch was at its height between 1790 and 1815, when up to 15,000 tons of gunpowder a year was detonated there. The result is a stupendous gulch, its sides aglow with orange and yellow tints.

As in the south Wales coalfield, so also elsewhere in Wales, expanding industry created a demand for cheaply and rapidly built housing. In the north and west too, much of the industry was located in the upland districts, at altitudes of between 650 and 820 feet (200 and 250m) on Halkyn Mountain, at Minera and at Blaenau Ffestiniog, and up to 1,300 feet (400m) in the lead mining districts of Cardiganshire and Montgomeryshire. Penybryn, a row of single-storeyed cottages built in the Ystwyth valley in about 1835 was typical of the housing of the upland lead miners. In towns, housing could be appallingly congested; an example is John Street, Bethesda. But as the quarrying districts had a strong tradition of combining slate-working with farming, many of those employed in the quarries lived in the agro-industrial dispersed settlements which are such a feature of upland Caernarvonshire. Those whose smallholdings were more distant lived during the week near the mine or quarry in 'barracks', like those in the Dinorwic Quarry. At Halton near Chirk the High Barracks was possibly a kind of lodging house. Perhaps the most interesting of the surviving examples of early nineteenth-century Welsh industrial housing are the weavers' houses built in the woollen towns of Montgomeryshire. Often three or four storeys high, the ground and usually the first floors formed the dwellings which were frequently built back-to-back.

Opposite: *Iron and coal were by no means the only nineteenth-century industries to scar the landscape of Wales. The great hole at the Penrhyn slate quarry, near Bethesda, was well under way by 1850 (Crown Copyright: The Royal Commission on the Ancient and Historical Monuments of Wales, 93-CS-1154).*

In the textile-working towns of mid Wales, many rows of houses were surmounted by open workshop floors or factory rooms. This row of small two-storey houses at 1-4 Union Street, Newtown is surmounted by one long upper floor, or factory room, designed for hand spinning or weaving (Jeremy Lowe).

The upper floor or floors were unpartitioned 'factory rooms' containing hand-worked looms. Scores of such buildings were erected at Newtown and Llanidloes between about 1820 and 1850; the Newtown Textile Museum is accommodated in a group of them, and one of the town's weaving quarters — Penygloddfa — is a conservation area.

The growth of industry, though revolutionary in its scale and its implications, was not sufficient, initially at least, to absorb the ever-growing population. Between 1780 and 1820, squatting on upland waste land reached epidemic proportions and the multiplicity of tiny peasant holdings nearly drove the rural Welsh to the abyss that overwhelmed the Irish. A typical squatter settlement was that at Trefenter on Mynydd Bach in Cardiganshire, where by the 1840s there were forty smallholdings on some 160 acres (65ha). Squatters' homes were constructed from whatever was at hand, as were the rest of the dwellings of the rural poor. In south-west Wales, they generally had clay walls, a form of building thought of by later generations as impermanent and a mark of shameful poverty, although modern ecologists consider them to be splendidly organic, and, with proper maintenance, very durable. Thatched and brightly painted, they existed in their thousands in Cardiganshire and Carmarthenshire as late as the first decade of this century. In much of the north, cottages were built of rubble, sometimes using stones of gigantic size. Along the borderland 'black-and-white' construction, abandoned by the gentry, continued among the peasantry at least until the early decades of the nineteenth century. In some areas, however, light frames covered with weatherboard were coming into fashion. Cottages progressively acquired fireplaces, glass windows, parlours, stairs, upper floors, dormer windows and additional service rooms, an evolution which exactly mirrored that of the yeomen's houses two or three centuries earlier.

Squatting was both a cause and a consequence of the enclosure movement, which also reached its climax between 1780 and 1820, a period when Parliament passed 106 bills relating to enclosures in Wales. Some of them —

Cottages of the early nineteenth-century rural poor in Wales were constructed of whatever material was to hand. Bwlchygarreg at Rhiw on the Llŷn peninsula is a classic example from the north-west. The rubble stone walls have massive boulders at their base, and the roof is covered in small slates — the cheapest output of the Snowdonian quarries (Jeremy Lowe).

those relating to the marshes at Saltney, Malldraeth and Morfa Rhuddlan, for example — led to the drainage of low-lying and potentially fertile land. Most of them, however, were concerned with high moorland, and the aim of their promoters was not the improvement of agriculture but rather the intensification of landlord rights. The most ambitious of the Acts were those passed in 1808 and 1815 dealing with the 40,000-acre (16,000ha) Great Forest of Brecon. It was blatant class legislation, for it deprived commoners of over half the grazing land to which they had previously had access and gave rich pickings to a few speculators. Scottish lowlanders leased much of the land allotted to the Crown and their homesteads, sheltered by belts of conifers, are still features of the landscape. Enclosure led to the building of further vast lengths of dry stone wall. In some areas, however, hedges were preferred, planted with quickthorn, or, occasionally, as in parts of Cardiganshire, with laburnum.

Enclosures were a major feature in the continuing growth in the size of the leading landed estates. Other factors — especially indebtedness among the smaller squires and the effect of partible inheritance practised by many yeomen farmers — also assisted the process. The Cardiff Castle estate of the Bute family increased in size by 25 per cent between 1790 and 1815, while vast sheep walks were added to the estates of Golden Grove, Faenol and Trawsgoed. The long war with France (1792–1802, 1803–1815) led to higher prices for agricultural produce, thus permitting landlords to demand higher rents. The fortunately placed among them could also benefit from the royalties and other profits yielded by industry. The increasing wealth of the landed élite was reflected in their building operations. While some of the new mansions remained faithful to the sober, harmonious traditions of the eighteenth century, the architectural eclecticism of the nineteenth meant that Wales, by 1850, had been endowed with country houses in a bewildering variety of styles. Romanesque was employed at Penrhyn, Gothic at Margam, Tudor at Stanage, Jacobean at Llanrhaeadr Hall, Greek at Clytha House, Islamic at Garth, and Dutch at Clyro Court. As Thomas Hopper put it: 'It is an architect's business to understand all the styles and to be prejudiced in favour of none'.

Hopper's work at Penrhyn Castle (1820–37) is the most prodigious fruit of this building boom. Financed by the profits of the Bethesda quarries, the castle, 625 feet (190m) long, has a vast keep, a grand staircase and a great hall, all awash with blind arcading, ribs and bosses, chevrons and billets. Although faithful in the main to the Romanesque, Penrhyn has some fourteenth-century features and much Arab-style ornament, for the historicism prized by later architects was not always apparent in the work of the early nineteenth century. Although Clytha House (about 1838) is learnedly Ionic, Margam (1830) is Gothick rather than Gothic, and the style employed at Garth (1809–15) was a very free interpretation of the traditions of the Moguls. Even stranger is Gwrych Castle near Abergele (1819–53); as much a gigantic folly as a dwelling house, its mixture of styles and its medley of towers and curtain walls surely make it Wales's most astonishing architectural agglomeration.

Thomas Hopper's gloriously Romanesque Penrhyn Castle of 1820–37 was financed by the profits of the Bethesda slate quarries. By 1850, Wales had been further endowed with additional country houses built in a bewildering range of styles.

Major landscaping and garden-making continued to appeal to the landowners of Wales in the period 1780–1850. The cult of the Picturesque was at its height, and there are few finer examples of its expression than the garden of the 'Ladies of Llangollen' at Plas Newydd. Among the features were these rustic steps illustrated in a nineteenth-century watercolour.

In the period 1780 to 1850, the landowners of Wales were even more prodigal in their landscaping activities than they had been in the mid-eighteenth century. The most extensive activities were those of Thomas Johnes (d. 1816) at Hafod in the Ystwyth valley. Between 1790 and 1811, he undertook a vast programme of afforestation; walks and bridges led to vantage points, and his estate was embellished with a cavern, pools, obelisks, fountains, summer-houses and gazebos. Johnes had links with Stanage Park near Knighton, where between 1803 and 1809 Humphry Repton (1752–1818) created scenic drives and lakes and directed a large-scale scheme of afforestation. The cult of the Picturesque reached its extreme at Llangollen, where the Ladies of Plas Newydd adorned a ravine with rustic steps and bridges, cascades and pools and banks of moss and ferns. More ambitious were the plans carried out at Middleton Hall above the Tywi valley; there an extensive landscape was transformed by an elaborate scheme of water management, producing waterfalls, pools, bridges, weirs and bathing buildings.

William Paxton of Middleton Hall also built Paxton's Tower, a splendid folly overlooking the Tywi valley. Folly-building was a characteristic activity of the age of the Picturesque. Ruined castles and abbeys were considered to be primarily follies, and William Gilpin (d. 1804) suggested in 1782 that Tintern Abbey could be made more delightfully irregular by the judicious use of a mallet. Grottoes, decorated with shells, were a favourite form of folly and examples survive at Talacre in Flintshire and at Pontypool Park. The usual folly, however, was a tower, often with pretensions to being a memorial. Wales's finest is the Anglesey Column (1817) at Menai Bridge, but there are other interesting examples at Deri Ormond, north of Lampeter, at Bryncir, north of Porthmadog and at Wynnstay. Some apparent follies may have had other purposes; the two towers built by the Bailey brothers at Nant-y-glo in 1816 were intended to cow the workers and to offer a place of refuge to the hated ironmasters. The oddest of Wales's follies is the Jubilee Tower erected in 1810 on the summit of the Clwydian Range; now in ruins, it was the earliest Egyptian-style monument to be built in Britain.

In the age of the Picturesque, ruined castles and abbeys were considered to be primarily follies. Tintern Abbey in the Wye valley was perhaps the most celebrated site, seen in this watercolour by Edward Dayes (1763–1804) from the English side of the river (The Whitworth Art Gallery, the University of Manchester).

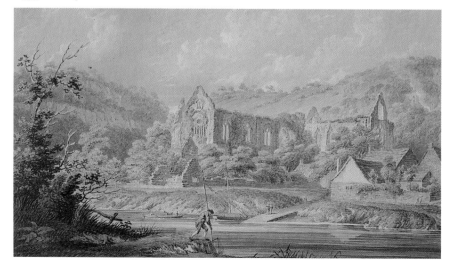

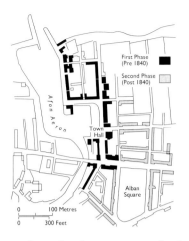

It was not uncommon for some estate owners of the first industrial era to create entire villages, and even towns. Aberaeron in Cardiganshire was created by the Gwynne family, and there is still a feeling of harmony among its stuccoed streets. The plan shows the two principal phases in the layout of the town, pre-1840 and post-1840 (After Hilling 1976).

Some landowners went further and created entire villages, and even towns. Marford near Wrexham, built between 1803 and 1815, is Wales's most charming estate village, and there are others at Merthyr Mawr, Aberriw and Llandegai. A more ambitious project was the industrial village of Morriston, begun by the Morris family in the 1760s; it had a grid-iron pattern of streets with a church at the main intersection, and the Morrises also built high-rise accommodation, the first block of flats in Wales. Two other landowners' projects, launched in 1807, had a more rural setting. The Gwynne family created the town of Aberaeron, with its harmonious, stuccoed streets, and W. A. Madocks (d. 1828) laid out the equally harmonious Tremadog and built the sea-wall which led to the rise of the town and port of Porthmadog. Madocks's hopes for a great port on the western seaboard had echoes in those of the Greville family, the founders of the town of Milford Haven. Between 1780 and 1809, three parallel streets were built above the haven and the Grevilles sought to make the town a major centre of shipbuilding, fishing and the transatlantic trade. The largest planned town created in Wales between 1780 and 1850 owed nothing to the enterprise of landowners. That town was Pembroke Dock; a naval dockyard was established there in 1814, giving rise to a community twice as large as that of neighbouring Pembroke. Laid out as a grid, Pembroke Dock contains some attractive early nineteenth-century features, although much of its single-storey housing was very modest indeed.

Side by side with the creation of new towns and the burgeoning of industrial settlements was the expansion of the older market towns of Wales, almost all of which at least doubled in size between 1780 and 1850. They also became safer and more salubrious, for paving, draining, lighting and policing were major concerns of early nineteenth-century civic authorities. While country houses were increasingly eclectic in style, town houses generally remained faithful to the scaled-down Palladian tradition. Much of the townscape created in Wales between 1780 and 1850 survives, and is often loosely described as 'Regency'. Among the highlights are Laura Place, Aberystwyth, Victoria Place, Haverfordwest, the Bulwark, Brecon, High Street, Llanfyllin, Salop Road, Welshpool and most of the towns of Tenby and Beaumaris. Other styles tended to be chosen for public buildings — neo-Tudor at the County Hall, Mold (1834), for example, and at the Town Hall, Flint (1840).

Established as a naval dockyard, Pembroke Dock was the largest planned town created in Wales between 1780 and 1850. Laid out as a grid, the town contains some attractive features. In the left foreground of this view is the star-shaped Defensible Barracks built in 1844–45 to protect the town and dockyard (Crown Copyright: The Royal Commission on the Ancient and Historical Monuments of Wales, 95-CS-1077).

Swansea's Royal Institution of South Wales is one of the more distinguished public buildings built in Wales in the first half of the nineteenth century. With its stately portico in the Ionic style, it is an elegant building of 1841.

Opposite: This charming group of church, school and master's house at Llangasty Tal y Llyn overlooking Llangorse Lake in Powys was built in 1848–50. The patron was Robert Raikes, an Oxford man influenced by the liturgical and architectural ideals of the contemporary Oxford Movement.

Among the most distinguished public buildings erected in Wales in the first half of the nineteenth century was the Town Hall at Bridgend (1843); impressively and austerely Doric, its demolition in 1971 was a sad act of philistinism. Equally Doric, but less austere, is the old shire-hall at Brecon (1842), now the Brecknock Museum, while the Royal Institution at Swansea (1841) is in the rather more elegant Ionic. Other public buildings of the period include hospitals, gaols, workhouses and educational establishments. The North Wales Mental Hospital at Denbigh (1848) is grandly Jacobean, while the town's gaol (1843) has handsome rusticated lintels. Forty-five workhouses had been built in Wales by 1850; some of them — that at Llanfyllin (1848), for example — have a certain charm, and the massive House of Industry at Forden (1795), capable of housing a thousand inmates, was, as a contemporary put it, 'a splendid receptacle of misery'. In 1850, Wales's boom years of school and college building had not dawned, but by then the country did have some not unattractive educational buildings, in particular Cockerell's work at Lampeter (1822–27), Ginell's at Llandovery (1848) and Prichard's at Cowbridge (1849–52).

The buildings at Lampeter and elsewhere were the product of the revival of the Church of England in Wales. By the 1850s, the Established Church was beginning to face up to the challenge represented by a growing and increasingly redistributed industrial population, although it was in the succeeding decades that the Anglican Church's building movement took off. Parliament's belief that the teachings of the Established Church were the antidote to the rebelliousness of the working classes led to government grants for church building. Some 'Commissioners' Churches' were erected in Wales, generally uninspired buildings typified by those at Buckley (1822), Glyntaff (1837), and Bagillt (1839). The growth of market towns led to the construction of

St David's College Lampeter, designed by Charles Robert Cockerell (d. 1863), pre-dates the boom years of school and college building in Wales (Crown Copyright: The Royal Commission on the Ancient and Historical Monuments of Wales).

churches such as St David's, Newtown (1847), built in a neo-Gothic mode unmindful of medieval proprieties. The wealth of the south Wales coalfield financed some churches of interest — St David's, Rhymney (1843), for example, the last neo-classical church to be built in Wales, and St Mary's, Cardiff (1845), an interesting exercise in Romanesque with Byzantine details. The Oxford Movement led to a deeper knowledge of medieval architecture, particularly that of the twelfth and thirteenth centuries, considered to be quintessentially the age of faith. The church at Llangorwen near Aberystwyth (1841) is an early product of the movement, as is the delightful ensemble of church, school and master's house at Llangasty on the banks of Llangorse Lake (1848–50).

But the first half of the nineteenth century was above all the period of the building of Nonconformist places of worship. Between 1800 and 1850 a new chapel was being opened in Wales on average every eight days, and many hundreds more were to be built in the following six decades. According to the Religious Census of 1851, chapel accommodation in Wales was sufficient to seat 50 per cent of the population, and in several districts, particularly in the rural north, the number of seats exceeded the number of inhabitants. Some of the chapels represented a departure from the oblong box tradition — Peniel, Tremadog (1811), for example, with its Tuscan columned portico, and Capel y Groes (1838), the octagonal chapel at Margam. Of those of a more traditional design, the simpler remained faithful to the practice of having the opening and the pulpit on the long walls. That was the layout of Capel Cymer (1834), one of the earliest chapels to be built in the Rhondda. Some chapels — Ramoth, Cowbridge (1828), for example — were square in plan and crowned by a pyramid roof, but the style increasingly favoured was the oblong with the opening in the gable façade. The early nineteenth-century façades were very simple and restrained. As Peter Segar has put it: 'If religion is based on the Word, never have God's houses been so parsimonious in their language'.

Between 1800 and 1850, a new chapel in Wales was being opened on average every eight days. The Ramoth Independent chapel of 1828 at Cowbridge was by no means exceptional, though its square plan crowned with a pyramid roof was not to retain great favour. The building is now the United Free Church.

The simplicity is deceptive. In much of urban Wales, the chapels offered the only evidence of anything approaching deliberately conceived architecture, and as Nonconformists were not concerned to ensure that their places of worship had an eastern alignment, their buildings fitted into the street scene better than did those of more ritualistic denominations. Although the only design elements in the façade were the relationship between doors and windows, the emphasis given to the pediment, and the placing, or otherwise, of an inscribed plaque, the variety offered by such an apparently restricted range of options was surprisingly large; so much so that, of the thousands of gable-façade chapels built in Wales, not one is an exact replica of another.

The years 1780 to 1850 were not only the era of the radical remaking of Wales; they were also a period when the Welsh landscape was recorded on a scale far fuller than ever before. The work of topographical artists, pioneered in the mid-eighteenth century by the Buck brothers, became vastly more plentiful; there can hardly have been a scene in Wales not drawn by the prolific Henry Gastineau (d. 1876). Landscape and seascape painters proliferated; Cyfarthfa Castle Museum at Merthyr has important depictions of the iron industry and the Glynn Vivian Gallery at Swansea houses fascinating paintings of the town's docks and shipping. Swansea has an honoured place in the history of photography, soon to become by far the most important medium for recording the making of Wales. Calvert Jones, a close associate of Henry Fox Talbot, was the town's rector, and in March 1841 Jones was responsible for what is probably the earliest example of photography in Wales — the beautiful daguerreotype of Margam Abbey now in the National Library at Aberystwyth. Topographical dictionaries of Wales were published — that of Carlisle (1811) and of Lewis (1833) — and in 1846 the first issue of *Archaeologia Cambrensis* appeared, the beginning of a systematic examination of the historic monuments of Wales.

Above all, the late eighteenth and early nineteenth centuries were the pioneer years of the Ordnance Survey, founded in 1791. The first task of the mapmakers was the creation of a system of triangulation which would allow a close survey of the entire kingdom from accurately located points. The triangulation of Wales was carried out between 1800 and 1820, when issues such as the exact height of Snowdon were settled. By the mid nineteenth century inch-to-a-mile maps covering almost the whole of the country had been published and by then the preparation of the 25-inch-to-a-mile maps was well advanced. Among the many merits of the Ordnance Survey maps is the fact that they provide a published record of thousands upon thousands of place-names, for one of the chief aspects of the making of a country is the way in which its inhabitants mark their land with names. Equally important as a source are the Tithe Maps and Apportionments prepared in the 1830s and 1840s, for they contain hundreds of thousands of field-names as well as offering an almost complete record of the use made of the land of Wales in the mid nineteenth century. This accumulation of knowledge was to become even more pronounced in subsequent periods, thus allowing the activities of the more recent makers of Wales to be documented with an unprecedented fullness.

The wealth of the south Wales coalfield financed a number of churches of interest including St Mary's in Cardiff's Butetown. Its design is an interesting exercise in Romanesque, coupled with Byzantine details.

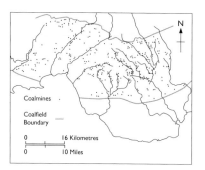

Coal mines in Glamorgan in 1913.

The complex at Navigation Colliery, Crumlin, was built between 1907 and 1911 by Partridge Jones and Company. It was a show-pit of the period, with high quality brick buildings and modern machinery.

THE SECOND INDUSTRIAL ERA

THE MAKING OF WALES 1850–1914

The remaking of Wales, apparent between 1780 and 1850, was consolidated between 1850 and 1914 — so much so indeed that Wales, perhaps to a greater extent than any other part of the United Kingdom is, in visual terms, a Victorian and Edwardian country. Over half its houses, the majority of its civic buildings, many of its churches and the great mass of its chapels are a legacy of the later nineteenth and early twentieth centuries.

By 1914, the Welsh economy was heavily dependent upon extractive industries, and the landmarks created by those industries dominated much of urban Wales. Above all, the coal industry of south Wales grew with extraordinary speed, fuelling steam engines and shipping around the world. As coal extraction took over from iron-making as the chief industry of the south Wales valleys, the pitheads with their winding-towers became a defining symbol of Welsh industrialization. Made of lattice steel and supported by elegant support struts and delicate arched trusses, they were structures of distinction, but they now survive only where coal production has been replaced by mining museums. Among other industrial constructions, the most interesting were the warehouse at Cardiff's East Bute Dock (1861), a building whose functional integrity is more characteristic of the twentieth than of the nineteenth century, the Weaver's Flour Mills at Swansea (1898), with claims to be the earliest reinforced concrete building in Europe, the Boiler Factory at Queensferry (1905), hailed by Nikolaus Pevsner as 'the most advanced British building of its date', and the complex at the Navigation Colliery at Crumlin (1911).

In the transformation of the landscape, industrial buildings were perhaps less significant than industrial refuse. By the early twentieth century, Wales was a land of tips. The most dramatic was the White Tip above Merthyr, the accumulated spoil of Dowlais's mining and iron working operations, but the largest was that at Bargoed, a vast, squat man-made mountain. Other Welsh

Nine pits were sunk at Ferndale and Tylorstown in the Rhondda between 1861 and 1907. In 1909 the nine pits were employing 6,826 men. This photograph of 1907 shows No. 6 and No. 7 pits, which were sunk by Alfred Tylor in 1873–76 (Welsh Industrial and Maritime Museum).

industries were more prodigal producers of spoil heaps. Every ton of slate created nine tons of waste, much of which still lies around Bethesda, Llanberis, Corris and Blaenau Ffestiniog. Quarrying had a greater impact upon the landscape than had coal mining. Until the advent of large-scale opencast mining, coal workings were out of sight. With the exception of Blaenau Ffestiniog, with its massive slate mines, slate-working was a surface activity. Above Llanberis, the giant steps carved out of the slopes of Elidir are breath-taking, and that is even more true of the deep amphitheatre at Penrhyn, near Bethesda. Almost as impressive are the workings on the north face of Yr Eifl, once a major source of granite setts. Lead and copper working produced more noxious waste. Nothing grows on the spoil heaps of the lead mines of Cardiganshire, Montgomeryshire and Flintshire, and by the early twentieth century copper smelting had wreaked havoc in the lower Swansea valley.

Essentially a surface activity, quarrying had an even greater impact upon the landscape than coal mining (Welsh Industrial and Maritime Museum).

117

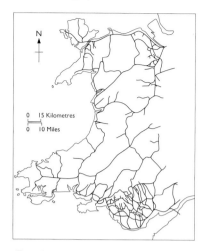

The railway network of Wales by 1914.

Railways and docks vied with industry in transforming the landscape. Between 1850 and 1870, around 1,400 miles (2,250km) of railways were constructed in Wales, a figure which had at least trebled by 1914. A high proportion of the lines were built to serve the south Wales coalfield, where rivalry between companies produced a particularly dense network of railways. Where a railway followed a valley, as did those of the pioneer companies of the coalfield, its construction offered few complications, although the gorge below Merthyr Vale was hard-pressed to contain two railway lines, a road, a canal and a tramroad, as well as the river Taff. Cross-valley lines, involving cuttings, embankments and viaducts, had a far greater impact. The Crumlin viaduct (1857), a 1,650 feet (503m) crossing of the Ebbw River supported on innovative iron trusses — now sadly demolished — was considered to be one of the engineering wonders of the later nineteenth century.

Elsewhere in Wales railways could have an equally striking impact, especially when they intruded into areas hitherto almost totally undeveloped — Talerddig, for example, with its dramatic cutting, or the Mawddach estuary with its appealing wooden viaduct. Some of Wales's most impressive railway structures were on lines serving routes already pioneered by canal and road builders. Thus, Robertson's viaduct at Chirk is cheek by jowl with Telford and Jessop's aqueduct, and Stephenson's railway bridges across the river Conwy and the Menai Strait complement Telford's masterpieces. The quarrying areas were served by a number of narrow-gauge railways, including that from Porthmadog to Blaenau Ffestiniog (1863), the earliest narrow-gauge railway in the world to use locomotion. Those that survive — the 'Great Little Trains of Wales' — are among the most attractive features of the landscape.

The second half of the nineteenth century was the great age of railway building in Wales. A high proportion of the lines were built in the south Wales coalfield, but elsewhere the new railways could be a striking feature in the landscape. In the foreground of this aerial view of the Menai Strait is the Britannia Bridge of 1845–50, designed by Robert Stephenson (d. 1859). It complements Thomas Telford's suspension road bridge of 1819–26 in the distance (Crown Copyright: The Royal Commission on the Ancient and Historical Monuments of Wales, 89-CS-623).

*Crumlin Viaduct.
Built by Kennard 1857.
Cost £62,000. Height 200 ft. Length 1658 ft*

The Welsh railway system, with its lack of major termini, was not endowed with magnificent stations. Some Welsh stations do, however, have considerable merit, especially the Italianate buildings serving the Chester and Holyhead Railway. That railway hugged the coast and thus had a marked impact upon the physiognomy of the northern coastal towns. At Colwyn Bay and Abergele, access to the seashore involves crossing the railway; at Flint, the line brutally disturbs the town's medieval layout and at Conwy it impairs the majesty of the borough's southern defences. Elsewhere, Wrexham was mauled by railway building, for much of its ancient centre was obliterated. Like Abergele, Barmouth and Aberdyfi were severed from the sea, and the linear town of Port Talbot suffered greatly from its bisection by the South Wales Railway. At Cardiff the railway was carried across the town on an embankment; a barrier therefore separated the docklands from the rest of the town, an obstacle with profound sociological implications. Railway building at Cardiff involved the diversion of the Taff and the creation of Wales's most renowned piece of real estate — Cardiff Arms Park. It also led to the creation within the town of vast areas of railway sidings accommodating trucks of coal awaiting shipment.

Road transport saw few innovative developments between 1850 and 1914, although the Transporter Bridge at Newport (1906) is a very rare species of river crossing. Transport by sea gave rise to massive constructions. Cardiff acquired five large docks, including the Queen Alexandra, hailed on its opening in 1907 as the largest masonry dock in the world. Large-scale dock-building also took place at Newport, Barry and Swansea, while Penarth, Port Talbot, Briton Ferry and Llanelli were endowed with at least a dock apiece.

The Crumlin railway viaduct built by T. W. Kennard in 1857 was considered to be one of the engineering wonders of the later nineteenth century (Welsh Industrial and Maritime Museum).

Newport's Transporter Bridge of 1906, a rare form of river crossing, was designed by F. Arnodin.

Elsewhere, port development was less extensive, partly because the growth of the railway network led to the decline of ports such as Haverfordwest and Cardigan, once the centres of a lively coastal trade. Slate export led to some construction work at Caernarfon, Bangor and Porthmadog, but in the north-east Mostyn was the only place to retain the shipping traditions of the Dee estuary. The most dramatic of Wales's maritime structures were the great breakwaters built at Holyhead and Fishguard; work at Fishguard was especially laborious, for the cliff face at Goodwick was torn down to accommodate the harbour.

But of all the achievements of the makers of Wales between 1850 and 1914, the greatest was to house the population, which rose from 1,189,000 to 2,523,000. The achievement was particularly marked in the industrial areas, where population increase could be phenomenal. Blaenau Ffestiniog's inhabitants doubled in number between 1851 and 1871; those of Mountain Ash trebled between 1871 and 1891, as did those of Mynydd Islwyn between 1901 and 1911; above all, there was the Rhondda, where the population increased seventy-seven-fold, from 2,000 to 154,000, between 1850 and 1914. The townscape of industrial Wales, particularly that of the south Wales coalfield, has been widely criticized. There was much to criticize, for the growing communities were urban but not civic; there was the monotony of the endless streets of terraced housing, the lack of public amenities and examples of gross congestion — in 1914 Tylorstown and Ferndale in the Rhondda Fach had a population density of 182 persons per acre (450 per ha).

Nevertheless, there were some positive aspects. Most of the urban development undertaken after 1850 was subject to by-laws which laid down the width of streets and the length of back gardens. As the century advanced, drainage, sewerage, pavements and lighting were progressively provided and, even in the most congested districts, the open mountainside was never far away. There was a strong tradition of owner-occupation, and therefore neglect by landlords was less of a problem in the south Wales coalfield than it was in districts where the vast majority lived in rented property. Indeed, many informed commentators considered that the south Wales miners were better accommodated than were those of the other major coalfields of Britain. Most of the houses of the south Wales valleys were built of local stone, with Pennant Sandstone dominating the central belt. Brick surrounds, often painted, came increasingly to be a feature of doorways and windows, as at Elliotstown at New Tredegar with its spectacular terraces. Other decoration of the façade was rare, although there are streets — at Llanelli, for example — rich in recessed arches, rusticated quoins and elaborate architraves. Parallel rows of double-fronted houses such as the Scotch Houses at Llwynypia (about 1865) had by the last quarter of the nineteenth century given way to two-sided streets with single-fronted houses. By then the typical coalfield house had evolved: three ground-floor rooms one behind the other, a passage-hall and three small bedrooms, a pattern repeated hundreds of thousands of times in the valleys of the south Wales coalfield, and prevalent too in the industrial areas of the north.

The eighty terraced houses of Stanleytown in the Rhondda were built in 1895 at a price of £166 each. The architect was T. R. Phillips of Pontypridd.

Opposite: *The population of the Rhondda increased from just 2,000 in 1850 to 154,000 in 1914. Housing the growing population was the greatest achievement of the makers of Wales at this time. This aerial view of the Rhondda Fawr looks north-west from Ton Pentre towards Treorci and Treherbert (Crown Copyright: The Royal Commission on the Ancient and Historical Monuments of Wales).*

Near the eastern edge of the south Wales coalfield, the miners' village at Oakdale was essentially a product of the garden village movement. It dates from 1909 to 1924, at the very end of the second industrial era (Crown Copyright: The Royal Commission on the Ancient and Historical Monuments of Wales, 905541-03).

The streets around Stow Hill in Newport provide a good example of a Victorian residential area. Indeed, many towns of Wales are rich in middle-class housing of this era.

Similar houses dominated the townscape of the ports serving the coalfield, as the mass of working-class houses at Newport, Cardiff and Swansea amply testifies. In the ports, however, the presence of a middle class created a demand for more elaborate dwellings, although they were often scaled-up versions of the coalfield house. Wales is very rich in Victorian middle-class housing. Earlier high-status houses tended to be near the town centre, but, as growth accelerated, there was a movement to more salubrious locations, a phenomenon nicely illustrated at Swansea; in 1851 the most privileged groups lived around St Mary's Church and the Royal Institution, but by 1871 they had migrated to the slopes of Townhill. Swansea has some excellent Victorian residential areas — the handsome stucco villas of Belgrave Gardens, for example. So does Newport, where the streets around Stow Hill are particularly attractive, and earnest seekers may find distinction at Neath, Llanelli and even Port Talbot. Above all, there is Cardiff, a cornucopia of Victorian delights. The differing layouts of the various sections of Cardiff depended upon whether they were in single or fragmented ownership — the former generally leading to a degree of conscious planning and uniformity in building design, and the latter to a miscellany of high density houses. The largest landowner at Cardiff was the marquess of Bute; his agents favoured the erection of middle-class houses in dignified streets often enhanced by public gardens, an example followed by most of the rest of the town's major landowners. Cardiff, it was complained, was too well built, for it had a chronic lack of modest dwellings within the reach of the lower-paid. The high quality of its residential areas may be appreciated in places such as Plasturton Avenue and the rows encompassing Roath Park. Above all there is Cathedral Road, a long avenue with a superb unity of design, though hardly any building is an exact replica of its neighbour. The walls are Pennant Sandstone, the mullions and transoms Bath stone and the façades are enlivened with gables, finials, lozenges and blind arcades, together with doorways topped by arches bewildering in their variety.

The streets of Cardiff present a cornucopia of Victorian delights. Above all there is Cathedral Road, a long avenue with a superb unity of design, yet with a bewildering array of Gothic detail in doorways and windows.

Llandudno is possibly the most handsome of all Welsh towns. The resort was laid out by the Mostyn family in the 1850s, with a desire to benefit from tourists brought in by the Chester to Holyhead Railway.

Beyond the confines of the south Wales coalfield and its ports, Welsh urban centres during the Victorian and Edwardian eras had a somewhat mixed history. The population of Wrexham quadrupled, but the towns which had once been Wales's most populous centres — Carmarthen, Haverfordwest, Brecon, Caernarfon, Denbigh and Welshpool — stagnated or even shrank. Seaside towns and spas experienced significant growth as trips and holidays became more common. The northern coastal resorts, easily accessible to the burgeoning population of Lancashire, expanded tenfold, while the resorts of the south and west coasts and the spas of mid Wales enjoyed considerable prosperity. The most imposing of the resorts is Llandudno, laid out by the Mostyn family in the 1850s with the intention of benefiting from the Chester to Holyhead Railway. With the fine sweep of its promenade, and flanked by the Great and Little Ormes, Llandudno is perhaps the most handsome of all Welsh towns. It has a wealth of ornate cast-iron arcading and also a splendid pier, one of the nine built in Wales in the late nineteenth century. Of the spa towns, the most interesting by far is Llandrindod, a coherent architectural assemblage in cheerful brick and enhanced by fine hotels and pretty woodland pavilions.

Despite accelerating urbanization, the majority of the inhabitants of Wales in the mid-nineteenth century were still country dwellers. Although those directly involved in cultivating the land had become a minority, farming continued to be the largest single source of employment. With a growing urban market for agricultural produce and increasingly effective means of distributing it, the prospects for agriculture seemed bright. By the early 1870s, 27 per cent of the cultivated land of Wales was under cereal, green or root crops, compared with 10 per cent a century later. 'High farming' involved heavy investment in drainage, fencing and manuring and led to the imposition of a new orderliness upon much of the countryside. The efforts of the improvers had some degree of success, but by 1880 cheap imports from America and Australasia were resulting in a deep agricultural depression.

In the 1880s, there was a massive flight from the land which, despite some recovery in the prices of agricultural produce in the early twentieth century, continued until the First World War.

Fluctuation in the fortunes of farming had implications for the landscape. During the era of 'high farming' there was considerable investment in farmhouses and outbuildings, with excellent building work done, for example, by the Grosvenor estate in Flintshire and the Bute estate in Glamorgan. The long impoverished counties of the south-west enjoyed a degree of prosperity. The 'great rebuilding', experienced in the borderlands between 1530 and 1640, took place in the uplands of south-west Wales between 1840 and 1880. 'To travel from Welshpool to Aberystwyth', states Peter Smith, 'is to pass from a seventeenth-century to a nineteenth-century landscape'. With the onset of agricultural depression rural depopulation accelerated, causing the population of many upland rural parishes to decline by 30 per cent and more between 1880 and 1914. Settlements on high-altitude marginal land were abandoned. As a result, districts such as the slopes of Plynlimon (Pumlumon) abound in the ruins of the dwellings of those whom the alternative of work in an industrial area caused to abandon the drudgery of seeking to wrest a livelihood from an inexorable environment.

The waxing and waning of income from agriculture was central to the ambitions of landowners. With the agricultural depression, the ability to build great houses and to manipulate the landscape became confined to those with non-agricultural sources of wealth. Landlords solely dependent upon agriculture were in increasingly straitened circumstances and some of them began disposing of their estates, a development with massive implications for the countryside.

The greatest of the landscape manipulators of Victorian Wales was the Liverpool banker, John Naylor, who between 1849 and 1874 spent a fortune on Leighton Hall and its estate, situated across the Severn from Welshpool. The house, a Gothic extravaganza decorated to designs by Pugin, was surrounded by vast gardens, enhanced by a viaduct, cascades and exotic trees; among them were the largest plantations of Californian Redwoods in Britain and the original of the Leyland cypress — named after Naylor's bank and now the great menace of suburbia. The features of the estate included a funicular railway, a network of piping to supply farms with liquid manure, a gasworks and channels to drive turbines and water-rams. It was Liverpool money too which permitted Henry Sandbach to build Hafodunos, east of the Conwy valley. Completed in 1866 and surrounded by luxurious grounds, it was one of the most interesting of the country houses designed by George Gilbert Scott (1811–78).

The wealth of the south Wales valleys financed the building or the acquisition of a number of country houses. None of them was within the coalfield, for coalowners lacked the ironmasters' desire to have a daily prospect of their enterprises. The houses included several in the Vale of Glamorgan, Hean Castle near Tenby, Glanusk near Crickhowell, Llanwern east of Newport, Plasdinam near Llandinam and Gregynog north of Newtown. Plasdinam (1874), designed by Eden Nesfield (1835–88), is an

The Home Farm at Leighton Hall was laid out in the mid-nineteenth century by a wealthy Liverpool banker, John Naylor. He spent some £200,000 on the farm and estate, founded on the firm belief of the efficiency in 'model farming'. The scale of the vast farm buildings can be appreciated in this aerial view (Crown Copyright: The Royal Commission on the Ancient and Historical Monuments of Wales, 93-CS-0747).

Gregynog, north of Newtown, has the appearance of a half-timbered mansion, though it is in fact built of concrete and dates to about 1860–70.

early example of the revival of the domestic building style of the Middle Ages, while Gregynog, although seemingly a superb half-timbered mansion, is in fact built of concrete. The most remarkable building enterprises financed by the coalfield's wealth were those of John, third marquess of Bute (1847–1900). Castell Coch, surely Wales's most delightful landmark, is a wonderful recreation of a thirteenth-century castle. Cardiff Castle represents the climax of the high Victorian dream; its turrets and spires are a splendid addition to Cardiff's skyline, and its interior has a sumptuous theatricality unmatched anywhere. The marquess's vast wealth permitted him not only to build, but also not to build. Cardiff's extensive open spaces, the city's greatest asset, survived unbuilt upon because their owner was rich enough not to be tempted by the wealth their exploitation could produce.

Designed by William Burges (d. 1881), Castell Coch in the Taff valley north of Cardiff is a wonderful recreation of a thirteenth-century castle.

Burges's earlier creation for John, third marquess of Bute, was Cardiff Castle — the climax of the high Victorian dream. The spires and turrets of the exterior enhance the capital's skyline, and the interior is sumptuously decorated and brimming with imagery. This view shows the grandly-named banqueting hall (Cardiff Castle).

The copper industry of Anglesey was the source of income which financed the building of Kinmel Park near Abergele. This gorgeous little gate lodge, the Golden Lodge (1868), was designed by Eden Nesfield.

The slate industry had financed the building of Penrhyn Castle, but in the second half of the nineteenth century the quarry-owners built little of distinction, apart perhaps from the interminable Faenol wall, once described as the longest folly in Europe. Anglesey's copper industry did bear architectural fruit, for the income from Mynydd Parys was the source of the wealth which financed the building of Kinmel Park near Abergele. In terms of architectural history, Kinmel was the most important building to be erected in nineteenth-century Wales. Designed by Eden Nesfield and completed in the 1870s, it is in the so-called Queen Anne style which evolved into the neo-Georgian style so widely employed in the early twentieth century. In that evolution, Nesfield's work is of seminal importance.

Kinmel had a room set aside for ironing daily newspapers, but by the time the house was finished the ability to maintain a lifestyle on such a scale was becoming increasingly difficult. By the early twentieth century, the building of great country houses had virtually come to an end; among the last to be erected in Wales was the huge new range of Llangoed Hall, south of Builth, designed by Clough Williams-Ellis (1883–1978) and completed in 1914. The attention of architects turned to medium-sized houses unattached to an estate and located as often as not in a suburb rather than in open country. Llanfairfechan boasts Bolnhurst (1899), the work of H. L. North (1871–1941), a perfect example of the 'Arts and Crafts' style. The most distinguished practitioner of the style was Charles Voysey (1857–1941) and his sole building in Wales is Tybronna (1903) on the Cardiff—St Fagans road. Interest in suburban 'country' houses went hand in hand with the *rus in urbe* movement which enjoyed widespread support in the early twentieth century, giving rise to garden villages at Wrexham (1901), Rhiwbina (1912–13), Swansea (1913) and Barry (1915).

Bolnhurst at Llanfairfechan was built in 1899 by Herbert Luck North (d. 1941), and is a perfect example of the 'Arts and Crafts' style.

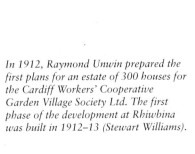

In 1912, Raymond Unwin prepared the first plans for an estate of 300 houses for the Cardiff Workers' Cooperative Garden Village Society Ltd. The first phase of the development at Rhiwbina was built in 1912–13 (Stewart Williams).

As country houses were scaled down, so also were gardens, and by the twentieth century the cottage-garden style pioneered by William Robinson and Gertrude Jekyll was widely popular. It represented a reaction against the bedding-plant layout much prized by Victorian gardeners. Wales once had many examples of the over-elaborate Victorian garden — at Baron Hill, for example, where scores of gardeners were in constant attendance — but as they were grotesquely labour-intensive, none of them has survived intact. Shrub and tree gardens have proved more durable. The most glorious of them is Bodnant, above the Conwy valley; begun in 1874 by the Lancashire industrialist Henry Pochin, it is one of the wonders of the world. Vastly enriched by the introductions of plant-hunters, Bodnant contains virtually every tree capable of flourishing in a temperate climate. Imported plants also featured in the splendid Japanese garden at Shirenewton east of Newport and at Dyffryn in the Vale of Glamorgan. Introductions, however, could have unfortunate consequences, for *Rhododendron ponticum* now infests large areas of upland Wales.

The development of the naturalistic gardens at Bodnant in the Conwy valley was begun by the Lancashire industrialist Henry Pochin. The terraces were created between 1904 and 1914 by his grandson, Henry Duncan McLaren (d. 1953), who was to become the second Lord Aberconwy.

Work on damming the river Vyrnwy began in 1881 and the lake was filled seven years later to provide water for Liverpool. The straining tower of 1881–92 is a remarkable structure and an outstanding achievement of Victorian water engineering.

By the end of the nineteenth century, ambitious gardening projects were being increasingly undertaken by public bodies rather than by private individuals. Roath Park at Cardiff was laid out in 1887 and municipal gardens were established at Newport, Aberdare, Neath and elsewhere. Landscape manipulation was also becoming far more of a public enterprise. The most scene-transforming activities were those of the water committees of major municipalities. Cardiff, Newport and Swansea constructed a series of reservoirs in the Brecon Beacons, some of them — Newport's at Talybont in particular — resulting in prospects of great beauty. Liverpool began damming the Vyrnwy river in 1881, Birmingham the Elan in 1882 and Birkenhead the Alwen in 1911. The Vyrnwy dam was the first large masonry dam to be constructed in Britain and the reservoir's straining-tower is a remarkable castellated structure rich in machicolations.

The proliferation of public buildings also emphasized the fact that, as the nineteenth century advanced, ambitious architecture was becoming confined to the public domain — the first time that that had been the case since the castle-building activities of King Edward I. The increasingly prosperous and money-orientated economy of Wales created a demand for shops, department stores and banks. The growth of industry and the export trade led to the erection of port offices and exchanges. Solidarity in the coalfield was expressed in workmen's institutes and leisure needs were served by libraries, theatres and public houses. Urban growth gave rise to town and market halls and, with the establishment of the county councils in 1889, county halls and offices were built. The rise of Welsh national consciousness had architectural implications, as did the late nineteenth-century boom in educational provision. The Anglican restoration and extension movement reached new heights and chapel construction continued unabated.

Cardiff's commercial centre was adorned in the late nineteenth century with a series of delightful shopping arcades. Castle Arcade, with its galleried first floor, was built in 1887.

In the wake of these developments, Wales was endowed with new buildings, many mediocre but some of undoubted quality. In the older market towns, the most striking transformation was the commercialization of the main streets. Shops whose windows had previously been glazed with small panes sprouted plate-glass ground-floor frontages, a development which destroyed the harmony of many a street scene. In places such as High Street, Welshpool, or Lammas Street, Carmarthen, those seeking to understand the townscape should direct their gaze to the upper storeys and to the backs of the buildings. The major towns acquired vast department stores — Ben Evans at Swansea, for example, and David Morgan at Cardiff — while Newtown was endowed with the remarkable Royal Welsh Warehouse (1872), from which one of the world's earliest shopping-by-post enterprises operated. Cardiff's wide burgages, the result of centuries of retarded growth, permitted the construction of delightful shopping arcades; Castle Arcade (1887), with its galleried first floor and its oversailing top storey is the most attractive. In the smaller towns the most obtrusive new buildings were the banks; in Great Darkgate Street, Aberystwyth, for example, Barclays (1877), National Westminster (1903) and Midland (1909) are on a scale wholly out of proportion with the rest of the street.

In the ports, banks could be even more monumental, as at Butetown, for example, or at Wind Street in Swansea. Swansea has some impressive port buildings, in particular the Harbour Trust Offices (1903) and the Exchange Buildings (1913–15). More imposing is the splendid Port Building at Barry (1898), with its beautifully symmetrical façade and its fine columned and pedimented bays. In Cardiff's docklands, where the Bute estate hoped a great commercial city would arise, there are several buildings of distinction, although the dignity of the original layout has been much undermined. Particularly delightful is the Pierhead Building (1896–97), an exercise in French Gothic carried out in brick and terracotta. The most grandiose is the Coal Exchange (1884–88), intended in the 1970s to be the seat of the proposed Welsh Assembly. Its pompous exterior offers little suggestion of the glories of the interior, where the main hall, reconstructed in 1911–12, is richly elaborate.

Cardiff's Pierhead Building was constructed in 1896–97 to a design by William Frame, who had been an assistant to William Burges at Cardiff Castle and Castell Coch. French Gothic influences are apparent, and all is raised in red brick and terracotta.

In the 1880s and 1890s, colliery development and its associated housing transformed the hamlet called Navigation into the mining settlement of Abercynon. The Workmen's Hall and Institute, built in 1904, was eventually to dominate the streetscape here. This striking building was sadly lost to the architectural heritage in 1995.

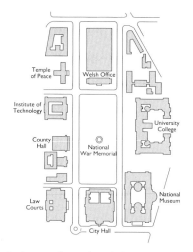

Cathays Park was bought by the Cardiff Corporation from the marquess of Bute in 1898. It has subsequently been developed to become the finest civic centre in the British Isles. The monumental buildings are set out in such a way that the qualities of each can be appreciated in its own right.

The City Hall in Cathays Park was built in 1901–05, to designs by E. A. Rickards. It is a building demonstrating the brilliance of its architect, and was to set a new standard in the emergence of great civic buildings in Edwardian Britain.

Within the coalfield, the most striking buildings, apart from the chapels, were the workmen's institutes. The largest building ever erected in the south Wales valleys must surely be the institute at Abercynon (1904), demolished in 1995, and a close rival is the Park and Dare Institute at Treorci (1895 and 1913), happily still standing. Of all the institutes of the coalfield, the most attractive is that at Blaenavon, now refurbished. The northern coalfield had its institutes too, with splendid Baroque examples at Llai and Rhosllannerchrugog. Libraries played a role not dissimilar to that of institutes. The Guest Memorial Library at Dowlais (1863), reputedly designed by Charles Barry, was among the earliest purpose-built libraries in Wales. Others followed, including the rather ponderous Cardiff Central Library (1882 and 1896), the neo-Tudor Gladstone Memorial Library at Hawarden (1902), the Art-Nouveau Free Library at Newtown (1902) and the many Carnegie libraries, among them excellent examples at Cathays in Cardiff and at Wrexham. Theatres, another aspect of the architecture of recreation, have had a more chequered history. At Swansea, where several theatres were built in the Victorian and Edwardian eras, only the Grand (1897) survives more or less intact. At Cardiff, with its less distinguished theatrical history, virtually the sole remnant of those eras is the attractive but sorely neglected façade of the Prince of Wales Theatre (1878). Aberystwyth can boast the fine Coliseum Theatre (1904), now the Ceredigion Museum, but the most appealing theatre built in Wales was Adelina Patti's miniature version of Bayreuth, erected in 1890 at Craig-y-nos in the upper Tawe valley. Public houses and hotels were at least equal to theatres as centres of recreation. Urban Wales is rich in fine nineteenth-century and early twentieth-century pubs, although the interiors of the majority of them have been thoughtlessly modernized. Some of the grander hotels have been turned over to other uses. In Aberystwyth, for example, the astonishing Castle Hotel became the University College, and the Queen's

Hotel was adapted as county offices. Many distinguished buildings, however, still fulfil their original function, including several at Llandudno, the Park Hotel at Cardiff (1884) and the Metropole at Llandrindod (1899).

Among Wales's municipal buildings, those of particular interest still in use include the town hall at Ruthin and the market halls at Mold and Abergavenny. The establishment of the county councils led to the erection of a diversity of buildings, varying from the unassuming Cardiganshire County Hall at Aberaeron to the Corinthian splendours of the Glamorgan County Hall at Cardiff. The Glamorgan County Hall is part of one of Europe's most splendid complexes of civic buildings. Cathays Park was bought by the Cardiff Corporation from the marquess of Bute in 1898 with the intention that the land should provide sites not only for buildings to serve Cardiff but also for those which would emphasize Cardiff's position as the largest urban centre in Wales. The most glorious of the buildings is the City Hall, designed by E. A. Rickards (1872–1920), an architect who deserves to rank among the pre-eminent makers of Wales. Completed in 1905, the year Cardiff became a city, its dome, capped by a wonderful dragon, and its clock tower, enriched by flamboyant convolutions, are the high points of a superbly harmonious and richly detailed masterpiece.

To the right of the City Hall stands the National Museum and Gallery, a more squat and streamlined building than its neighbour but in some ways more aesthetically pleasing. It was begun in 1910, a year before work started on the National Library at Aberystwyth. The museum and the library can therefore be considered the first Welsh national buildings ever erected. Yet perhaps it could be argued that Wales's institutions of higher education were equally national in their motivation. The University College, Aberystwyth, the cradle of the Welsh national revival, was opened in 1872. It had to make do with J. P. Seddon's exotic hotel, but at Cardiff and Bangor purpose-built colleges were erected. The first section of the college at Cardiff, completed in 1909, was a worthy neighbour of the other sculptured white buildings in

Opened in 1863, the Guest Memorial Reading Room and Library at Dowlais, Merthyr Tydfil, was among the earliest purpose-built libraries in Wales.

The courtyard ranges of the main building at the University College of North Wales, Bangor, were built between 1907 and 1911, to designs by Henry T. Hare. It is one of the city's most splendid landmarks.

The Education Act of 1870 laid down that elementary school should be within reach of every child, and in turn this led to a flurry of school building. In rural areas the new schools often became the focal points of communities. In urban industrial areas the schools of this era could be vast. Manselton Primary School, Swansea, was built in 1901–02, and had over 1,200 pupils.

Cathays Park; sadly its library, the most beautiful room ever built in Wales, has suffered the indignity of having its lower storey floored over, with the result that its superb harmony has been ruined. The Cardiff College also acquired a building in Newport Road, a section of whose proposed quadrangle was completed in 1915; now an incongruous remnant, it represented the last fling of neo-Gothic in Wales. Bangor was particularly fortunate in its initial building; the fine uncluttered complex designed by H. T. Hare (1860–1921) and opened in 1911 provides the city with a splendid landmark. Of all Wales's university buildings, the most appealing is the smallest — the University Registry in Cathays Park (1904), cheerfully squeezing in among its monumental neighbours.

Educational provision at the primary and secondary levels had far greater implications for the landscape. The Education Act of 1870, which laid down that an elementary school should be within reach of every child, led to a flurry of building. As much of rural Wales lacked villages, the location chosen for the school often became the focal point of the community, a phenomenon particularly observable in parts of Cardiganshire, Anglesey and the Llŷn peninsula. Late nineteenth-century rural schools, with their high windows, railed playgrounds and often crowned by a belfry, are significant features of the landscape. In the industrial areas, the rate of school construction could be very rapid; seven were built in the Rhondda between 1878 and 1881, and a further twenty-eight by 1901. Urban schools could be vast. Terrace Road School, Swansea, built in 1888, accommodated 1,455 children; Manselton School, also in Swansea, contained 1,212 pupils and is, as John Newman has put it: 'An ingenious and dramatic composition, worthy of an Elizabethan prodigy house'. Following the passage of the Welsh Intermediate Act in 1889, the building of county schools began and ninety-five had been completed by 1905. In many rural towns, the county school was by far the largest complex of buildings and by acquiring one the town immediately moved to the apex of the local urban hierarchy.

While School Boards were ensuring that every child was within reach of a school, the Established Church was seeking to ensure that the whole population was adequately served by Anglican churches. During Bishop Ollivant's episcopate at Llandaff (1849–82), 170 new churches were built in the diocese and at least an equal number were restored or enlarged. In the vast diocese of St Davids, where centuries of neglect meant that hundreds of churches were in semi-ruin, rebuilding became such a passion that in many areas — central Cardiganshire, for example — it is difficult to find a church containing any features earlier than the 1850s. The four cathedrals were thoroughly restored, with St Davids and Llandaff in particular undergoing vast refurbishment. In 1863 the west front of St Davids was rebuilt to the somewhat bland Romanesque design of George Gilbert Scott; at Llandaff the arcades were reconstructed, the nave roofed and a splendid south tower and spire built, giving the cathedral an air of consequence it had previously lacked. The work at Llandaff was mainly that of John Prichard (1817–86) of Llangan, an example, rare until the twentieth century, of a native of Wales designing major projects in his own country. Among the highlights of the Anglican

The later nineteenth century was to see a new boom in Anglican church building. The best-known example in Wales is probably the so-called 'Marble Church' of St Margaret at Bodelwyddan. It was an estate church, built at the expense of Margaret, Lady Willoughby, as a memorial to her husband. Constructed in 1856–60, the architect was John Gibson (d. 1892).

St Augustine's, Penarth, was designed by the great Victorian architect William Butterfield (d. 1900). At the time of its construction in 1865–66, Butterfield was at the height of his career, and here he produced a wonderful example of the polychrome genre so fashionable at the time.

rebuilding were broach spires — at Canton, for example, or Sketty, or Llanrhystud or Llanddarog — and chunky coalfield churches such as the dramatically sited Christ Church at Aberbeeg. Architecture employing the juxtaposition of materials of different colours, enjoyed a great vogue, with St Augustine's (1866) at Penarth a classic example of this polychrome genre. G. E. Street (1824–81), the most tireless of the architects of High Anglican churches, designed at Tywyn, near Abergele, a superb grouping of church, vicarage and school. Just 3 miles (4.8km) from Tywyn stands the best-known of all nineteenth-century Welsh churches, St Margaret, Bodelwyddan, an exercise in indiscriminate opulence.

The Anglican building campaign, though vigorous, was vastly exceeded by the efforts of the Nonconformists. By 1905 there were 1,229 Nonconformist places of worship in Glamorgan, a threefold increase since 1851; the Rhondda had 150 chapels, a number of them capable of accommodating over a thousand worshippers. In the middle decades of the nineteenth century, chapel architects were generally loyal to the tradition of the restrained pedimented gable façade, typified by Siloa, Aberdare (1855) or Tabernacl, Pontypridd (1861). Some chapels, however, acquired dignified classical porticoes — the superb Bethesda, Mold (1863), for example — or dispensed altogether with the pediment, as with the handsome Tabernacle, Cardiff (1865). As the century advanced, elaboration became increasingly prized; Tabernacl, Morriston (1873), the most monumental of all Welsh chapels, with its clock

tower and its gigantic Corinthian pillars, is splendidly idiosyncratic. Façades became wilder, with disconcerting hybrids such as Tabernacl, Cardigan (1870), Capel y Crwys, Cardiff (1899) and Rehoboth, Holywell (1904). Welsh-language congregations emphasized the distance between them and the Established Church by not espousing Gothic, although there are some exceptions, such as Pembroke Terrace, Cardiff (1877), Woodland Road, Colwyn Bay (1879) and Ebenezer Newydd, Swansea (1896). English-language congregations had no such inhibitions and most of the places of worship they erected after about 1870 tended to be humbler versions of Anglican churches. However, some of their buildings, that of the Presbyterians at Roath Park in Cardiff (1899–1901), for example, are of considerable distinction. Roman Catholics too were Nonconformists and their buildings include what are now the three Roman Catholic cathedrals of Wales — Our Lady of Dolours, Wrexham (1857), St David's, Cardiff (1884–87), and St Joseph's, Swansea (1888) — all designed by the firm of Pugin and Pugin.

By the late nineteenth century, church and chapel building had become an almost exclusively urban activity, for as a result of rural depopulation, the countryside was more than adequately supplied with places of worship. The growing urbanization of the population led to changed attitudes to the landscape, for rural people see the countryside as a source of livelihood, while townspeople see it as a source of recreation. Visits to the uplands of Wales, undertaken by a few intrepid seekers of the Picturesque in the late eighteenth century, had, with the growth of the railway network, become a mass activity. Places sprouted new names — Artists' Valley, Happy Valley, Torrent Walk and Panorama Walk. And it was land along Panorama Walk above Barmouth — the 5 acres (2ha) of Dinas Oleu — that became in 1895 the first property acquired by the newly-established National Trust. The age of the preservation of the landscape had arrived.

The age of the preservation of monuments, or, to use the current term, of built heritage, had also arrived. The Ancient Monuments Protection Act of 1882 laid the foundations for what a later age would call safeguarding the physical remains of the past activities of human beings. The Royal Commission on the Ancient and Historical Monuments of Wales was established in 1908 and by 1914 it had published five county inventories, although their quality was poor compared with the Commission's more recent publications. The state began to involve itself more closely with the care of the built heritage. Some of Wales's greatest monuments — the castles at Caernarfon and Harlech, for example — had always been Crown property, but of the other great Edwardian castles, Conwy had been sold in 1627 and Beaumaris in 1807. The Crown's purchase from the duke of Beaufort of Tintern Abbey in 1901 inaugurated a new policy. Acquisitions and those buildings already in the possession of the Crown eventually became the responsibility of the Office of Works, thereby launching a new era in the history of the safeguarding of the built heritage of Wales — although in subsequent decades the definition of built heritage was to snowball to an extent which would have totally confounded the late nineteenth-century pioneers.

The later nineteenth century saw the dawning of the age of the preservation of ancient monuments and historic buildings. Tintern Abbey, for example, was bought by the Crown in 1901, and the long process of conserving the ruins after centuries of neglect began.

WAR AND DEPRESSION

THE MAKING OF WALES 1914–45

For the people of Wales, as for the rest of the peoples of combatant Europe, the First World War was a devastating experience. Yet, as no part of Wales was bombed, the townscape of Wales suffered less than it would during the Second World War, although that war, for the Welsh, was much less of a blood-letting. Had the war not occurred, employment in the south Wales coalfield would probably have peaked in 1913. The industry had already overexpanded; the war and the post-war boom led to continued production, thus ensuring that the slump, when it came, was far more severe. The full implications were not apparent until 1925; in that year severe depression set in, resulting in the unmaking of industrial communities which had been in the making for a century or more.

In the countryside, the impact of the war was more immediately visible. The agricultural depression of the late nineteenth century had led to a collapse in high farming; by 1914, the proportion of the cultivated land of Wales under cereal, green and root crops had fallen to 15 per cent. Because of the need to have more home-produced food, the proportion had risen to 26 per cent by 1918, thus altering, temporarily at least, the appearance of significant areas of the countryside. More long-term in its effects was the war-time belief that Britain was overdependent upon timber imports. By 1914 only 5 per cent of Wales was wooded, a figure which represented the culmination of millennia of assarting. The establishment of the Forestry Commission in 1919 began a reversal of the process, for between 1919 and 1995 the amount of Welsh land devoted to commercially managed woods increased sixfold. There were criticisms that the Commission was undermining the viability of upland holdings and that its straight-edged plantations, mainly of Sitka Spruce, did nothing to beautify the landscape. The Commission's work transformed extensive areas of Wales, above all perhaps in the south Wales coalfield, where a forest now stretches almost unbroken from Margam to Rhigos. Along with suburban plantings of exotica, twentieth-century afforestation has made Wales one of the few countries the majority of whose trees belong to non-indigenous species.

By the eve of the First World War, the
coal industry had already overexpanded,
with the conflict and subsequent boom
encouraging yet further growth. In
1925, when the slump and depression
set in, the effects on industrial
communities were devastating. At
Ferndale in the Rhondda, closures began
in the 1930s (Welsh Industrial and
Maritime Museum).

The war strengthened the belief, already held by some landowners, that owning an estate was no longer a viable business. Between 1918 and 1922 at least a quarter of the landlord-held farms of Wales were placed on the market and most of them were bought by their tenants. By 1922, 35 per cent of Welsh farmers were freeholders, compared with 10 per cent before the war. The process continued over the following decades; by 1970, 64 per cent of the agricultural holdings of Wales were owned by those who farmed them, and by then the Welsh landed class, which had dominated the countryside since the late Middle Ages, was virtually extinct. Pride in achieving freehold status is movingly expressed by a monument in a field at Ambleston north of Haverfordwest to John and Martha Llewellin, who 'by the blessing of God on their joint undertaking and thrift, bought this farm and hand it down without encumbrance to their heirs'. Land reformers had argued that the removal of landlordism would bring about a rural renaissance, but the decline in the prices of agricultural produce from the early 1920s onwards meant that the possibilities open to the new class of freeholders were very limited; indeed, it was not until the 1950s and 1960s that the landscape implications of the emergence of the new class became apparent.

The landscape implications of the decline of the old class became apparent much earlier. Great gardens became overgrown, park walls began to collapse, as, in some cases, did the mansions themselves — Baron Hill, for example, and Hafod and Bronwydd. A number of stately homes were adapted to serve new purposes, Wynnstay becoming a school, Bodysgallen a hotel and Kensington Castle a hospital. Others eventually found security under the wing of the National Trust, in particular Chirk, Penrhyn and Plasnewydd. The suddenness of the collapse should not be overstated; the fourth marquess of Bute (d. 1947) held on to his vast park at Cardiff throughout the inter-war years and also undertook a vast restoration project at Caerphilly Castle, and between 1928 and 1937 the American tycoon, W. R. Hearst, spent a fortune refurbishing St Donat's Castle.

Following the establishment of the Forestry Commission in 1919, the amount of commercially managed woods in Wales increased sixfold by 1995. The effects on vast swathes of the Welsh landscape is only too readily apparent, especially across the south Wales coalfield.

The old order did not entirely collapse overnight, and there was always the unexpected. The American tycoon W. R. Hearst, for example, spent a fortune refurbishing St Donat's Castle in the Vale of Glamorgan.

While the post-war land sales were leading to profound changes in the countryside, post-war social legislation was initiating profound changes in the towns. The appointment of Christopher Addison as Britain's first Minister of Health in 1919 led to legislation permitting the government to give subsidies to local authorities to build houses. Council houses brought about a revolution in the housing of the working classes. The major ports seized the opportunity avidly. Between the wars, Newport rehoused half its population, Cardiff was active at Ely and elsewhere, and Swansea built the much-praised Townhill estate. Wrexham, where some municipal housing schemes had been undertaken before the war, was particularly progressive, and considerable building was also undertaken in the Deeside towns. Under the influence of the *rus in urbe* movement, inter-war municipalities aimed at low-density housing with semi-detached rather than terraced dwellings, extensive gardens, trees and grass verges. Their schemes were therefore prodigal in terms of land use; the built-up area of Newport doubled during the inter-war years, although the town's population grew by less than 10 per cent. In the more favoured parts of Wales, the 1920s and 1930s also saw much building of private housing, some of it in the stockbroker-Tudor and bypass-variegated styles beloved of cartoonists (Lisvane in Cardiff, Swansea's Gower Road and the suburbs of Colwyn Bay come to mind), but such developments were as nothing compared with the huge building boom in inter-war south-east England.

Very little building took place in the countryside, although overcrowded houses were more a rural than an urban phenomenon. Fear of spending paralysed the rural local authorities, dominated as they were by the limp remnants of the Liberal tradition. The local authorities in the coalfield were far more vigorous, but after 1925 they made few additions to the housing stock, for the region was increasingly seen as a worked-out mining camp. Little effort was made to correct its housing deficiencies until the 1950s and 1960s when it became apparent that, as a result of the inaction of the inter-war years, many valley communities had intractable problems. As the depression worsened, the image of a worked-out mining camp became increasingly apposite. Of the great ironworks, Cyfarthfa closed in 1921, Blaenavon in 1922, Ebbw Vale in 1929 and most of Dowlais in 1930; parts of the works were demolished, but many buildings of rich historical significance were left to fall into ruin. Between 1923 and 1928, coal output tonnage declined from 54 million to 35 million in the southern coalfield, and from 3.4 million to 2.7 million in that of the north. Winding-towers, washeries and coking-plants were abandoned by the score, thus adding to the scene of desolation.

The collapse of the prosperity of the south Wales coalfield had repercussions beyond its boundaries. The decline in coal exports dashed the hopes that Butetown would become a great commercial centre. Its finest building, the National Provincial Bank, was completed in 1927; thereafter, the district fell into depression and, in places, into semi-ruin until the 1980s when a vast renewal project was launched. Docks at Cardiff and elsewhere became idle and eventually several of them were filled in or became marinas. The extensive areas devoted to coal sidings were no longer needed and thus many acres became available for redevelopment. With the colliers' purchasing power

From the late eighteenth century onwards, much of the coal for the Cyfarthfa Ironworks at Merthyr Tydfil was grabbed from seams on the slopes of Mynydd Aberdâr. Ironstone, too, was quarried from this site. Such landscapes are fast disappearing as the land is reclaimed (Crown Copyright: The Royal Commission on the Ancient and Historical Monuments of Wales).

The decline in coal exports through the port of Cardiff dashed all hopes of Butetown becoming a great commercial centre. Its finest monument to the aspirations of the age is the National Provincial Bank, completed in 1927.

severely cut, disaster struck the woollen industry of west Wales, and in the Teifi valley mill after mill became derelict. Depression also struck the spa towns of mid Wales causing places such as Llanwrtyd to have a strongly melancholic air.

Yet it would be wrong to present the inter-war years solely as a tale of woe and to describe their impact upon the landscape exclusively in terms of the spread of dereliction. Although unemployment reached horrendous levels, there were always more families with earners than without, and the deflation of the period meant that those with steady incomes found their purchasing power increasing year by year. The number of private motor cars in Wales rose from 29,000 in 1926 to 81,000 in 1938, the beginnings of a revolution in mobility which would have revolutionary implications for the landscape. The coming of the lorry meant that bricks, tiles and corrugated iron could be carried cheaply to districts far away from a railway, districts which had formerly made extensive use of local materials in building. 'By 1930', Peter Smith has written, 'the last vestiges of real regional architecture had finally been destroyed'. Bus services proliferated, breaking down the age-old isolation of rural communities. Charabanc excursions allowed trippers to visit areas hitherto untouched by tourists — the further reaches of the Llŷn peninsula, for example.

Iron-making at the Cyfarthfa works in Merthyr Tydfil began in 1766, and by the first decades of the nineteenth century it was the largest ironworks in the world, employing about 1,500 workers. The site eventually closed in 1921 (Welsh Industrial and Maritime Museum).

Picture palaces became the quintessential architecture of the 1920s and 1930s. Although somewhat mauled in an unsympathetic age, the cinemas designed by Colwyn Foulkes at Flint and Rhyl testify to the talents of this spirited architect. There is also a good selection of work by Foulkes in Colwyn Bay, including this once delightful shop.

By 1933, the Central Electricity Board had established its power grid. Thereafter, vast areas of otherwise striking landscape were to become dotted with massive pylons.

Opposite: *The holiday village at Portmeirion in Gwynedd is surely the most charming group of buildings anywhere in Wales. The Italian style village was the invention of Sir Clough Williams-Ellis and was begun in 1926.*

Greater mobility and the relative affluence of considerable sections of society brought about a marked increase in holiday-making, a development which led to the laying out of Barry's Cold Knap and to extensive improvements at Porthcawl, Rhyl and Llandudno. For the less affluent, there were the caravan parks which were becoming major features of the coastlands of Flintshire, Denbighshire and Glamorgan. More elegant delights awaited the affluent. Among them was the holiday village which Clough Williams-Ellis began constructing at Portmeirion in 1926, surely the most delightful group of buildings anywhere in Wales. Portmeirion is architecture as entertainment and is proof that tourism does not necessarily ruin a landscape; indeed, it can enhance it.

Other developments did less, perhaps, to enhance the landscape. The coming of broadcasting to Wales in 1923 led to the festooning of enthusiasts' houses with aerials and eventually to the erection of skyscraper transmitters and to the construction of that eyesore below the Breiddin, the Post Office's International Maritime Radio Station. The Central Electricity Board, established in 1926, had by 1933 constructed its grid, initiating the process which was to ensure that wide areas of Wales — the Vale of Glamorgan in particular — offered constant views of massive pylons. Wales seemed tailor-made for hydro-electricity, a development which began with the construction of the Trawsfynydd Lake and the Maentwrog turbine in 1930. The inter-war years too were the period of the creation of the basic telephone network, giving rise to a fascinating wirescape and ensuring that every rural road was bordered by an endless line of wooden crosses.

Of all the technical innovations which won widespread acceptance in the inter-war years, the most important was the cinema. Picture palaces were the quintessential architecture of the 1920s and 1930s, with the construction of such splendours as the Carlton in Swansea and the Capitol (now destroyed) at Cardiff. It was in the north-east, however, that cinema building reached its peak with the spirited work of Colwyn Foulkes (1884–1971). Foulkes is second only to Percy Thomas (1884–1969) among the architect makers of

The Welsh National War Memorial in Cathays Park, Cardiff, was designed by Sir Ninian Comper. A work of 1924–28, it is a beautiful and reverent classical composition.

twentieth-century Wales; several of his best works have been demolished and those that survive have been mauled, but the Plazas at Rhyl and Flint still testify to his talent. Foulkes left his mark on other aspects of the townscape of north-east Wales — at Station Road and Abergele Road, Colwyn Bay, for example. However, the main town-centre development of the inter-war years was the erection of shop fronts for chain stores, building work which ensured that the commercial core of any town came to look very similar to that of any other.

The construction of places of worship, a leading form of building activity over the previous 900 years, took place very rarely in the Wales of the 1920s and 1930s. Some interesting Catholic churches were built — the Church of the Resurrection at Ely, for example — but the erection of Nonconformist chapels virtually came to an end and the Anglicans undertook little apart from a remarkable project at Brecon; the elevation of the priory church of St John to the status of a cathedral in 1923 led to the refurbishment of the adjoining conventual buildings, thereby creating an ensemble of great charm. There were reverent aspects to one of the most distinctive activities of the 1920s — the erection of war memorials. Bangor acquired an impressive memorial arch and Cardiff the circular colonnaded Welsh National Memorial; most towns and many villages were provided with some form of commemoration, on occasion work by distinguished sculptors such as Goscombe John (d. 1952). The anti-war movement inspired the Temple of Peace, opened in 1938 at Cathays Park; designed in a streamlined classical idiom, it was one of the major 1930s commissions of the firm of Percy Thomas.

The same firm was responsible for the most splendid building of inter-war Wales — the Guildhall at Swansea. Also in the 'stripped classical' style, its restrained tower and its subtle massing of white cubes make it a building of great distinction; its quality can be appreciated by comparing it with the broadly contemporary county hall at Newport, where a not dissimilar design is handled with far less assurance. The inter-war years also saw the completion of the first phases of two buildings which had been begun before the war — the National Museum (1927) and the National Library (1937). The praises of the museum have already been sung. The library, designed by S. K. Greenslade, is perhaps too squat for its width, but it crowns the hill above Aberystwyth with great panache.

The National Library and the Temple of Peace were the last major buildings to be opened in Wales before the country was again involved in war. As during the First World War, the Second led to a vast expansion in arable farming and a further undermining of the lifestyle of what remained of the Welsh landed class. By 1939, the threat of war had already had an impact upon the Welsh landscape with the construction of a 'bombing school' at Penrhos, west of Pwllheli, and of an air base at St Athan in the Vale of Glamorgan. With the outbreak of hostilities, further military installations came to Wales, among them aerodromes at Fairwood, near Swansea, and at Valley, near Holyhead, a gunnery range at Castlemartin and camps at Tywyn, Trawsfynydd and elsewhere. Above all, a 40,000-acre (16,000ha) firing range was established west of Brecon, resulting in the pulverising of the seven

Swansea's Guildhall, designed by Percy Thomas and built in 1932–36, is the most splendid building of inter-war Wales.

beautiful valleys of Mynydd Epynt. Pillboxes and concrete barriers to hold back tanks were erected, some of the first significant fortifications — apart from some efforts in the Milford Haven — to be constructed in Wales since the castles of the Middle Ages. A military hospital was set up at Morriston and a gigantic munitions factory at Bridgend and other centres of armament production were established at Marchwiail, Glascoed, Hirwaun and elsewhere.

The locations of the war factories were chosen in part because it was believed that Wales was too far to the west to be subject to German bombing. The belief proved to be ill founded. At Llandaff, a land mine fell near the cathedral in 1941 and once again the building was in ruins. Elsewhere in Cardiff, bombs destroyed much of the area north of the General or Central Station and large sections of Butetown. Newport, Pembroke Dock and parts of Deeside were also bombed, but by far the greatest sufferer was Swansea. In the three-night blitz of 19, 20 and 21 February 1941, the entire town centre was obliterated. Further raids followed, including a ferocious one in February 1942, and when the war came to an end Dylan Thomas's 'ugly lovely town' was a disembowelled wreck.

The period 1914 to 1945 represented for Wales the years of the locust. The economic growth of the previous century had come to a halt and there was little hope of addressing the environmental problems industrialization had caused. The momentum of efforts to provide Wales with buildings to sustain its social and cultural life had been stalled. The traditional framework of rural communities had been undermined. In 1945, the makers of Wales faced a huge challenge. The transformation of the country in the following half-century is a measure of their success.

Bombs fell on a number of locations in Wales during the Second World War. By far the greatest sufferer was Swansea, but large sections of Cardiff's Butetown were destroyed. This view shows the aftermath of a blitz in Bute Street in April 1943 (Welsh Industrial and Maritime Museum).

Hospitals, leisure centres, libraries, swimming pools, theatres and stadiums are among the more notable public buildings built in Wales since the war. Of them, the most prized is the Welsh National Stadium of 1968–83. Its massive concrete supports dominate the central Cardiff skyline. It is to be replaced with a new millennium stadium as the process of the making of Wales continues into the twenty-first century.

THE RECENT PAST

THE MAKING OF WALES 1945–1995

Since 1945, the making, the unmaking and the remaking of Wales have proceeded at a wholly unprecedented pace. Large areas of the country, rural and urban, have been transformed, and even in the remotest districts few viewpoints can offer scenes identical with those of fifty years ago. Change has perhaps been more profound in the countryside than in the towns. One of the major problems facing the Labour government elected in 1945 was the inadequacy of the food supply. The Agriculture Act of 1947 brought in an array of subsidies, grants and deficiency payments which ensured that the Second World War, unlike almost all previous wars, was not followed by a depression in farming. In the post-war years, agriculture was the miracle industry of Wales. Although the percentage of the employed population directly dependent upon the land halved, output in most sectors of farming doubled.

The increasing efficiency of farmers was one of the chief keys to the transformation of the countryside. Innovation in agricultural practices meant that traditional farm buildings became redundant, and farmers, less hampered by the planning restrictions than were other entrepreneurs, erected buildings wholly out of character with their surroundings. Tall silage holders sprouted throughout dairying country, giving the slightly myopic traveller the impression that every settlement had acquired a church tower. Increased productivity called for the tearing out of hedges, an activity which altered the appearance of the traditional Welsh bocage, and also posed a threat to wild life. Improved farming methods involved heavy use of fertilizers, thus giving rise to pollution problems. The investment in machinery could only be justified if the holding was enlarged, and thus farm amalgamation proceeded apace. In 1945, Wales had about 40,000 farms in the full sense; fifty years later it had less than half that number, and a large proportion of the rural housing stock had been released for purposes other than agriculture. The process was aided by the continuing rise in freehold farming, which meant the

The twentieth century has seen new farm buildings sprouting across the Welsh landscape. Sadly, like the tall silage holders of dairy country, these are often wholly out of character with their surroundings.

absence of the restraints inherent in the estate system. Estates maintaining old landed families living off their rents were virtually extinct by the last quarter of the twentieth century, but new landlords were emerging — the National Trust in the upper Conwy valley, for example, or pension funds holders in the Vale of Tywi.

With their increasing income, farmers could modernize their dwellings. In the 1960s, there seemed to be a cement-mixer outside every farmhouse as occupants replaced mud walls, filled in wide fireplaces and installed metal windows, activities which robbed thousands of Welsh farmhouses of their historic meaning. Adventitious rural dwellers — those who lived in the countryside not because they had an economic role there, but because they chose to do so — constituted the majority of Wales's country dwellers by the late twentieth century, a social change of deep significance. They, too, modernized their houses, and they tended to prettify them as well, thereby adding twee touches which could be highly incongruous. A high proportion of the new rural dwellers were migrants from outside Wales. Some of them were anxious to live in houses whose names they could pronounce; thus Berllan Dywyll became Dark Orchard and Carreg-lwyd Greystones — ancient title deeds were being cast into oblivion.

By the 1980s, farmers were beginning to reap the penalties of their success. With surpluses accumulating and the costs of agricultural incentives rising, production quotas were introduced, the cause of deep resentment, especially in the dairying areas of the south-west. Farmers were paid not to farm. Set-aside came into vogue, thus endowing the countryside with patches of land which were in the process of reverting to an older untended condition. Diversification became the order of the day. By the 1990s, those who could recall the quasi-subsistence agriculture which had shaped the appearance of much of rural Wales fifty years earlier were viewed as survivors from a prehistoric age.

The modernization of historic farmhouses and cottages has gone on at a rapid pace since the 1960s. In the past, such modernization has sometimes robbed dwellings of their historic meaning. The new rural dwellers of recent decades have also increased this pace of modernization.

Between 1952 and 1976, Wales acquired eight more major reservoirs. Llyn Clywedog Dam was begun in 1964 and stands as the tallest mass of concrete in Britain.

The transformation of the countryside, in part the result of the increasing productivity of farming, was also promoted by other pressures, most of them emanating from the fact that the population of Wales, and of Britain, was overwhelmingly urban. One of the chief needs of those populations was an adequate water supply. Between 1952 (Claerwen) and 1976 (Brenig), Wales acquired eight major reservoirs, a development which aroused considerable controversy. Some of the engineering work was very impressive; the Llyn Clywedog Dam, the highest mass of concrete in Britain, has hollow buttresses with vaults which soar higher than those of any cathedral. The development of the electricity industry also involved considerable manipulation of the Welsh landscape. Hydro-electric complexes were erected above Blaenau Ffestiniog, in the Rheidol valley and, most notably, in the bowels of Elidir Fawr where the waters of Llyn Marchlyn and Llyn Peris are used with great ingenuity. Nuclear-powered stations were constructed at Trawsfynydd and Yr Wylfa; the former has now been decommissioned, but the latter, a splendidly monumental building improbably sited in the top corner of Anglesey, is still in operation.

The greatest pressure on the countryside was caused by the demands of recreation and tourism. Diversification primarily meant providing facilities for visitors. Butterfly centres, fish farms and pony-trekking centres proliferated and the number of golf courses soared. In much of rural Wales it seemed that the national motto was 'Bed and Breakfast', and many farmers found it preferable to milk fewer cows and more caravanners. Holiday camps became a significant feature of the landscape, not only at traditional resorts but also in wholly rural areas such as Penychen near Pwllheli, where Billy Butlin turned a wartime training establishment into a major holiday complex. Nature trails abounded and, with the urge to explain everything, ever-larger and grander interpretation centres sprang up. The most famous beauty spots came under threat as tens of thousands of boots pounded the paths up and down Snowdon and Cadair Idris.

In recent decades, immense pressure has been placed on the most famous beauty spots of Wales by the demands of tourism. The Snowdon Mountain Railway was opened as early as 1896 and is now one of the major tourist attractions in Wales.

Modern roadbuilding came to Wales with the construction of the M4 motorway. The scheme included the construction, in 1966, of the elegant and innovative Severn Bridge.

Central to the influx into the countryside was the growth in the private ownership of motor cars. The number of Welsh families owning cars increased tenfold between the late 1950s and the late 1970s, and the increase in the more prosperous regions of England was even greater. The implications for the landscape were immense. Hitherto uncluttered streets were henceforth lined with parked vehicles; petrol stations became a recurring feature of the roadside and housing developments were obliged to cater for garages and increased access roads. Until the 1960s, drivers had to make do with the existing road system, the cause of enormous traffic jams in places such as Port Talbot. Modern roadbuilding came to Wales with the construction of the M4, which included the elegant and innovative Severn Bridge (1966). Other distinguished examples of road engineering include bridges over the Dee at Queensferry and over the Cleddau near Neyland, ingenious flyovers at Newport and Briton Ferry and sections of the dual carriageway between Cardiff and Merthyr. Congestion at Conwy led in 1958 to the construction of a bridge which had a disastrous impact upon the prospect of the castle and decanted a mass of vehicles into the centre of the town; mercifully, a tunnel beneath the Conwy river has now been constructed. Compared with some English cities, Wales's major urban centres have not suffered greatly through road construction; a plan in the 1960s to drive an expressway through Cardiff was abandoned and access to Newport has been skilfully handled. Elsewhere, Caernarfon has been badly sliced, but other towns, Brecon, Llanidloes and Denbigh, for example, have been provided with bypasses which offer attractive urban views; a number of Welsh towns, however — Aberystwyth, Carmarthen and Llangollen among them — remain plagued with through traffic.

The vast hanger at Cardiff Wales Airport, Rhoose, must rank among the country's most obtrusive buildings. It is visible from most of the Vale of Glamorgan.

The great transport innovation of the post-war years was mass air travel. While British centralization means that most Welsh air travellers fly from airports near London, Wales does have one airport capable of handling international flights. Rhoose is now able to handle jumbo jets and even Concorde, while its vast hangar, visible from most of the Vale of Glamorgan, must rank among the country's most obtrusive buildings. The great transport regression of the post-war years was the contraction of the railway system. The scale of closures following the publication of the Beeching Report in 1963 meant that, by the late 1960s, Wales had a smaller railway network than it had had in the late 1860s. Abandoned lines came to be among the major features of the landscape; some poignant memorials remain — the tunnels in the Aberglaslyn Pass, for example, and the incline down the Clydach Gorge and the splendid viaduct above Cefncoedycymer.

Railway closure was as much a feature of industrial as of rural Wales, for, with the attenuation of the coal industry, the network of lines in the south Wales coalfield was unnecessarily dense. The saleable coal output of the south Wales ports declined from 24 million tons in 1952 to less than a million by the 1990s, and the number of major collieries contracted from 135 to just one. The Welsh Development Agency and the National Coal Board proved to be more conscientious than the ironmasters had been in clearing up the detritus of a dying industry; at Cwmfelin-fach, for example, there are few signs that the Nine Mile Point Colliery ever existed. Nevertheless, the south Wales coalfield, as is that of the north, is rich in the relics of its major industry, many of them more interesting than the rather sanitized monuments preserved at the Big Pit in Blaenavon and the Heritage Centre in the Rhondda. In landscape terms, the major development in the Welsh coal industry in the later twentieth century was the marked expansion in opencast mining. The excavations created by the 'sunshine miners' — that above Dowlais, for example, or those in the anthracite districts — represent landscape manipulation on a grand scale, and are a cause of much distress to communities in their vicinity. However, when the work is finished and the top-soil replaced, the new landscape can be very attractive. New landscapes were also created by the removal of tips — at Gelli-ceidrim in the Loughor valley, for example, where a

New landscapes have been created by the removal of colliery tips, such as here at Maerdy in the Rhondda (Crown Copyright: The Royal Commission on the Ancient and Historical Monuments of Wales).

handsome rounded hill replaced a scene of desolation. Tip clearing accelerated following the appalling disaster at Aberfan in 1966, with much of the waste at Aberfan being carried to Cardiff to fill in the West Bute Dock — the spoil of an industry being used to obliterate the transport facility which gave it birth. As the coal industry declined, the rivers of the coalfield revived, with trout in the Cynon and herons fishing in the Llwyd below Garndiffaith. The greatest reclamation project was that in the lower Swansea valley, where land poisoned by centuries of copper-smelting was detoxinated and replanted.

The contraction of employment in the coalfield had long given rise to demands that alternative work should be provided. Some efforts were made in the late 1930s with the re-establishment of steel-making at Ebbw Vale and the creation of a trading estate at Treforest near Pontypridd. After the war, such efforts redoubled. Architecturally, the most interesting result was the rubber factory at Brynmawr; consisting of a series of low domes, the building looked as if the Festival Hall had wandered to the slopes of Gwaun Helygen and had pupped.

Other distinguished factory buildings erected since the war have had a more fortunate history, among them the Pilkington factory at St Asaph, Anglesey Aluminium's complex near Holyhead and Anacomp at Brynmawr. Government initiative has endowed Wales with massive if rather undistinguished buildings, in particular the Royal Mint at Llantrisant and the licensing centre at Swansea. With the revival of the Welsh steel industry, the country has acquired the vast plants at Port Talbot and Llanwern, although rationalization has meant the demolition of works at Shotton, Ebbw Vale and Cardiff. Steelmaking at Port Talbot led to the construction of an iron ore terminal capable of handling ships three times the size of those able to gain entry to the older docks. Terminals in the Milford Haven can handle even larger ships — the huge tankers supplying the oil refineries which now line the haven's shores. The clusters of oil storage tanks erected on both sides of the haven come as a shock to those visiting the extremities of Pembrokeshire, constituting as they do an industrial landscape unique in Wales.

Developments at Milford Haven were in part intended to serve the petrochemical industries which were transforming the shores of Baglan Bay. Primarily, however, they came into existence to satisfy the demand for petrol for private vehicles. The growth in car ownership gave rise not only to vast

Designed in 1946–51, the Brynmawr rubber factory was built to bring aid to the devastated economy of the south Wales valleys. It was undoubtedly a spectacular building of its age, but following its closure in 1982 it was abandoned and allowed to fall into ruin. The factory was to become an object lesson in the problems of conservation. This view shows the building as completed in 1951 (The Architectural Press).

Opposite: *Swansea was at the heart of early industrial development in Wales, though by 1945 the copper industry of the Swansea valley had reached terminal decline. The city, too, had suffered major bomb damage during the war. In the past three decades, it is a city which has remade itself. This aerial view shows the rejuvenated docks and maritime quarter (Crown Copyright: The Royal Commission on the Ancient and Historical Monuments of Wales, 91554-14).*

road-building schemes but also to changes in housing provision and settlement patterns. Adventitious rural dwellers multiplied chiefly because of the car, ownership of which also led to the suburbanization of villages — in the Vale of Glamorgan, for example, or at Abergwili near Carmarthen or Bow Street near Aberystwyth. Wales's most interesting experiment in post-war town planning resulted from the challenge represented by the car. The Queen's Park housing estate at Wrexham was the first example of Radburn planning in Britain; pioneered at Radburn, New Jersey, the aim was to segregate pedestrian from vehicular traffic. The Wrexham scheme was carried out in the 1950s, and versions of it had been laid out in many parts of Wales by the late twentieth century. The same thinking inspired the pedestrian-precinct movement which has significantly enhanced Commercial Street, Newport and the Queen Street and St John's areas of Cardiff. Unfortunately the movement arose too late to affect Wales's largest town-planning scheme of the immediate post-war years — the rebuilding of Swansea. The decision to construct a dual carriageway through the middle of Swansea created a wholly disastrous townscape. The car too was the key to the construction of out-of-town shopping centres, with their pagoda-like buildings capped with vaguely ecclesiastical towers. Seen as a dire threat by town-centre traders, they have the capacity — as the experience of the United States has shown — to revolutionize the relationship between a town's core and its periphery.

Town planning became subject to severe criticism in the later twentieth century, partly because of some misconceived housing schemes but chiefly because of the extensive demolition carried out in the 1960s and 1970s. In that period, Merthyr lost two market halls, the iron bridge, the Triangle, Dowlais House, Dowlais School, Penydarren House and Brunel's railway station. In Cardiff the Franciscan priory was built over and the heart of Butetown was ripped out. In Caernarfon the walled town was disembowelled and at Conwy there were demands that Telford's bridge should be pulled down. Tudor Street and Flannel Street vanished from Abergavenny, one of the many market towns to suffer despoilation.

Of all the post-war building activities, the most massive was the addition to the housing stock. The cessation of building during the war, coupled with losses through bombing, meant that by 1945 there was a severe housing crisis. Lack of resources meant that a sustained attack on the problem had to be delayed, but pre-fabs offered a stop-gap solution. From the mid 1950s, council house construction took off with the building of extensive estates such as Penlan, Swansea, Betws, Newport and Llanrumney, Cardiff. Every market town acquired estates, some of them very banal, but others — those at Newtown and Beaumaris in particular — showing considerable imagination. In the south Wales coalfield, housing reached up into the moorland, thus blurring the old contrast between the built-up areas and the open mountain. Penrhys between Rhondda Fawr and Rhondda Fach was perched at an altitude of 1,300 feet (400m), as were Gyrnos and Galon-uchaf in Merthyr. Wales, however, was not overendowed with those disasters of the 1960s, high-rise council blocks, although a group of them was built, astonishingly, on the wide expanse of the Hirwaun moor.

Council estates built in the 1950s consisted almost invariably of virtually identical family houses, but in later decades a greater variety of dwellings was constructed. Among them were flats, a form of housing that the Welsh had hitherto shunned. Flats multiplied too in the older built-up areas as substantial houses at Cardiff and elsewhere were carved up. By the 1990s, very few of the houses of Cathedral Road were occupied by a single family. The post-war years have also seen the mushrooming of estates of privately-owned dwellings; public and private enterprise together have caused the housing stock of Wales to expand by 50 per cent since 1945, although the population has risen by only 15 per cent. Some of the private estates — Killay, near Swansea, for example — were very modest, but others could be lavish. Increasingly the houses were provided with integral garages, which presented major problems in creating a harmonious façade. Centrally heated, most of them lacked the chimneys which were the crowning glory of almost every house built before the later twentieth century. In the rural areas, the most obtrusive development was bungalow building; the inhabitants of mid Cardiganshire, like those of the west of Ireland, were avid bungalow lovers, the result, perhaps, of an atavistic desire to revert to the single-storey cabins of their ancestors.

Where public buildings were concerned, the makers of late twentieth-century Wales built nothing comparable with the original buildings of Cathays Park or the Guildhall at Swansea. The most striking achievement was the Welsh Office designed by Alex Gordon and Partners, a building with a splendid inner court, but remarkable in that nothing of Wales can be seen from its windows. The reorganization of local government led to the construction of not unattractive county offices, in particular those of Clwyd, West Glamorgan and South Glamorgan. County architects have been responsible for some attractive schools, among them the secondary schools at Llanidloes and Llanrwst. With the growth of higher education, the university colleges have built extensively; some of the best work was designed by the firm of Percy Thomas, which was also responsible for the BBC's Welsh headquarters at Llandaff.

Crematoria, virtually unknown in Wales before the war, have proliferated since 1945, with significant implications for the landscape, for the popularity of cremation has meant that there is no need to devote further land to cemeteries. Outstanding among the crematoria is that at Coychurch (1970). With the adoption of cremation, the commemorating of the dead with tombstones, a practice with millennia of history behind it, went into rapid decline, and it seems unlikely that future generations will lay out fascinating places such as the vast graveyard above Treorci. Hospitals, leisure centres, libraries, swimming pools, theatres, concert halls and stadiums are among the other major public buildings Wales has acquired since the war. Of them, undoubtedly the most prized is the Welsh National Stadium (1968–83), formerly Cardiff Arms Park, the massive concrete supports of which dominate the skyline of central Cardiff. Plans for a waterfront opera house, if realized, would allow Wales's capital to be able to boast an even more dramatic building by the end of the millennium.

West Glamorgan County Hall in Swansea was one of the new local authority buildings which followed the reorganization of 1974. Situated on the town's sea-front, it was built in 1979–84.

EPILOGUE

Writing of the English landscape in 1955, W. G. Hoskins commented that every change it had undergone in the recent past 'has either uglified it or destroyed its meaning or both'. Although the countryside of Wales has not been assailed as vigorously as has that of much of England, anyone who has seen Epynt or Freshwater East or Morfa Rhuddlan cannot but agree that Hoskins's comment has relevance in the Welsh context. Yet, partly because of the anguished cries of people like Hoskins, the natural heritage and the built heritage of Wales are better appreciated and better cared for in the 1990s than they were in the 1950s. The National Trust now safeguards extensive stretches of the Welsh coastline and Cadw can claim to be far more active than its precursor a generation ago. Almost 20 per cent of Wales lies within National Parks; the country also has three designated areas of outstanding natural beauty as well as a host of sites of special scientific interest. The Museum of Welsh Life at St Fagans offers a splendid display of Welsh regional styles and among its treasures are buildings which would have disappeared had they not been re-erected there. Merthyr, once so cavalier towards its history, has admirably restored the Dowlais stables, and throughout urban Wales handsome façades are now preserved and developers are obliged to reconstruct behind them, as at Wrexham's Wynnstay Arms and Cardiff's neo-Venetian Queen's Chambers and Cathedral Road synagogue. Yet it should be remembered that conservation can become nothing more than resistance to all change. We should never ask when Wales was made, for Wales is always in the making.

One of the newest features of the Welsh landscape — the windfarm. This example is near Llandinam in Powys (Crown Copyright: The Royal Commission on the Ancient and Historical Monuments of Wales).

FURTHER READING

Michael Aston, *Interpreting the Landscape* (London 1985).

Helen Burnham, *A Guide to Ancient and Historic Wales: Clwyd and Powys* (London 1995).

A. Caseldine, *Environmental Archaeology in Wales* (Lampeter 1990).

R. J. Colyer, *The Welsh Cattle Drovers* (Cardiff 1976).

F. G. Cowley, *The Monastic Order in South Wales 1066–1349* (Cardiff 1977).

John Davies, *A History of Wales* (London 1993).

R. R. Davies, *Conquest, Coexistence and Change: Wales 1063–1415* (Oxford 1987).

Wendy Davies, *Wales in the Early Middle Ages* (Leicester 1982).

Nancy Edwards and Alan Lane, editors, *The Early Church in Wales and the West* (Oxbow Monograph 16, Oxford 1992).

F. V. Emery, *The World's Landscapes: Wales* (London 1969).

R. A. Griffiths, editor, *Boroughs of Mediaeval Wales* (Cardiff 1978).

R. Haslam, *The Buildings of Wales: Powys* (Harmondsworth 1979).

John B. Hilling, *Cardiff and the Valleys* (London 1973).

John B. Hilling, *The Historic Architecture of Wales* (Cardiff 1976).

W. G. Hoskins, *The Making of the English Landscape* (London 1955).

Edward Hubbard, *The Buildings of Wales: Clwyd* (Harmondsworth 1986).

Stephen Hughes, Brian Malaws, Medwyn Parry and Peter Wakelin, *Collieries of Wales: Engineering and Architecture* (Aberystwyth 1995).

G. H. Jenkins, *The Foundations of Modern Wales: Wales 1642–1780* (Oxford 1987).

A. H. John, *The Industrial Development of South Wales 1750–1850* (Cardiff 1950).

Anthony Jones, *Welsh Chapels*, 2nd edition (Stroud 1996).

W. Linnard, *Welsh Woods and Forests: History and Utilization* (Cardiff 1982).

Thomas Lloyd, *The Lost Houses of Wales*, 2nd edition (London 1989).

Jeremy Lowe, *Welsh Industrial Workers Housing 1775–1875* (Cardiff 1977).

Jeremy Lowe, *Welsh Country Workers Housing 1775–1875* (Cardiff 1985).

Frances Lynch, *A Guide to Ancient and Historic Wales: Gwynedd* (London 1995).

K. O. Morgan, *Rebirth of a Nation: Wales 1880–1980* (Cardiff 1981).

Chris Musson, *Wales from the Air: Patterns of Past and Present* (Aberystwyth 1994).

V. E. Nash-Williams, *The Early Christian Monuments of Wales* (Cardiff 1950).

John Newman, *The Buildings of Wales: Glamorgan* (London 1995).

D. Huw Owen, editor, *Settlement and Society in Wales* (Cardiff 1989).

Oliver Rackham, *The History of the Countryside* (London 1986).

Mark Redknap, *The Christian Celts: Treasures of Late Celtic Wales* (Cardiff 1991).

D. M. Rees, *The Industrial Archaeology of Wales* (Newton Abbot 1975).

Sian Rees, *A Guide to Ancient and Historic Wales: Dyfed* (London 1992).

William Rees, *An Historical Atlas of Wales from Early to Modern Times*, 3rd edition (London 1967).

Stephen Rippon, *The Gwent Levels: The Evolution of a Wetland Landscape* (CBA Research Report 105, York 1996).

Peter Sager, *Wales* (London 1991).

M. Seaborne, *Schools in Wales, 1500–1900: A Social and Architectural History* (1992).

P. Smith, *Houses of the Welsh Countryside: A Study in Historical Geography*, 2nd edition (London 1988).

Ian Soulsby, *The Towns of Medieval Wales* (Chichester 1983).

J. A. Taylor, editor, *Culture and Environment in Prehistoric Wales* (Oxford 1980).

David Thomas, editor, *Wales: A New Study* (Newton Abbot 1977).

Elisabeth Whittle, *The Historic Gardens of Wales* (London 1992).

Elisabeth Whittle, *A Guide to Ancient and Historic Wales: Glamorgan and Gwent* (London 1992).

E. Wiliam, *Historical Farm Buildings of Wales* (Edinburgh 1986).

Glanmor Williams, *The Welsh Church from Conquest to the Reformation*, 2nd edition (Cardiff 1976).

Glanmor Williams, *Recovery Reorientation and Reformation: Wales c. 1415–1642* (Oxford 1987).

M. Williams, *The Making of the South Wales Landscape* (London 1975).

INDEX